I
Power

GEORGE DIETER has a Masters degree in the psychology of coaching, a Masters degree in psychology, and a law degree. He is currently the principal psychologist at a private practice specialising in relationship, child and adolescent counselling. George has presented papers at national and international conferences, as well as authoring a publication on issues confronting the juvenile justice system.

This book provides a refreshing new take on concepts like 'self', 'me' and 'boundaries'. George Dieter challenges traditional thinking with new perspectives that redefine the neural networks in new directions. His conceptualization leads to new insights in understanding conflict, relationships and ultimately self-empowerment. He moves smoothly between big picture concepts and neuroscience — from cognitions to emotions and how a strategy for life can be found in a fresh understanding of the self.

— **Dr Pieter Rossouw, School of Psychology, University of Queensland; Director, Institute for Neuropsychotherapy**

I

Power

The freedom to be *me*

GEORGE DIETER
MA (Psych), MA (ApplSc)

EXISLE
PUBLISHING

First published 2015
Exisle Publishing Pty Ltd
'Moonrising', Narone Creek Road, Wollombi, NSW 2325, Australia
P.O. Box 60–490, Titirangi, Auckland 0642, New Zealand
www.exislepublishing.com
Copyright © 2015 in text: George Dieter
George Dieter asserts the moral right to be identified as the author of this work.

A CiP record for this book is available from the National Library of Australia.

ISBN 978-1-921966-83-5

Cover design by Mark Thacker of Big Cat Design
Internal design and typesetting by Nick Turzynski of redinc. book design
Typeset in Newzald 11/16
Printed in China

This book uses paper sourced under ISO 14001 guidelines from well-managed forests and other controlled sources.

2 4 6 8 10 9 7 5 3 1

Disclaimer
While this book is intended as a general information resource and all care has been taken in compiling the contents, neither the author nor the publisher and their distributors can be held responsible for any loss, claim or action that may arise from reliance on the information contained in this book. As each person and situation is unique, it is the responsibility of the reader to consult a qualified professional regarding their personal care.

CONTENTS

Introduction

Imagine the following scenario. A man, let's call him James, is driving home late one evening from work when he suddenly has the urge to buy his partner a bunch of flowers. But not just any flowers. Something tells him it has to be a particular bunch of flowers (possibly some subliminal advertising taking effect). So he goes out of his way to find exactly the flowers he believes will have an extraordinary effect on her, and tell her just how much she means to him. He's happy to spend the time and effort — and fork out an exorbitant amount of money.

James arrives home and hands his partner the material representation of his love. And then, out of the blue comes her response. Well, not quite out of the blue — a hurt look clouds her face. *Uh oh. This wasn't in his mental script...*

'You know I don't like mixed flowers ... how many times do I have to tell you?' She's looking suspicious. 'What have you been up to? Why are you suddenly bringing me flowers anyway?'

This isn't going the way he imagined, at all.

'Nothing! I, um, I just thought you'd like them,' he replies. Now he's hurt too.

Put yourself in James' place — and then in his partner's. How would you have felt had this happened to you? Deflated? Angry? Frustrated? Misunderstood? All those feelings put together sound familiar? Perhaps you've experienced something similar — and yet James did exactly what he intended. He thought about buying some special flowers because he loved his partner, and eagerly handed them to her, as soon as he arrived home, just as he imagined. So why would James be anything but satisfied, since he's accomplished everything he set out to do? Surely he should be happy? Instead he feels the opposite. His partner is sobbing on the phone to her mother and his precious flowers are stem up in the rubbish.

This scenario is a classic example of how we can rely on someone else to make us happy, when no one can actually 'make' us happy — in fact, *nobody can make us feel anything.* We're each responsible for the way we feel and for how we respond to the situations we face on a daily basis.

When we surrender control of our emotions to someone else, understandably we feel out of control — and this feeling can contribute to us feeling stressed, anxious or even depressed.

In this book I'll explore these ideas from a neuropsychological perspective and show you how understanding that *you're* in control of your own emotional responses (that is, understanding where you end and another person begins — having a grasp on boundaries) can help you regain a sense of control over your emotions and find a path to better relationships and greater contentment. My focus will be on situations that give us grief, cause us distress and lead to dysfunction in the form of anxiety, depression or stress, and cause dissatisfaction in our relationships — even if only with ourselves. I'll highlight a particular aspect of human needs that may provide you with a roadmap to happiness — whatever that may mean for you.

Rather than simply discussing why I believe boundaries play such a significant role in our daily interactions, I rely on what we know about certain brain structures and their role in how we function as human beings. Understanding these structures also provides the answers to why we behave and react in certain ways — ways that may later create a source of frustration and bewilderment, in ourselves as much as in others. As a practising psychologist with the benefit of a few years of hindsight, I also take into account the findings psychological research has revealed over the past hundred years.

The book is divided into two parts. In **Part 1: The basic principles** we take a detailed look at the idea of boundaries and explore what this term really means. To demonstrate the connection between exercising control — what I call I-Power — and experiencing emotional relief, which forms the basis of the psychology of boundaries, I'll briefly outline a few basic mechanisms in the brain and the way they're organized. These simple explanations will make it easier for you to understand why boundaries aren't just psychological or philosophical concepts to help us understand and navigate the world, but also part of the process of how the more primitive part of the brain reacts to incoming stimuli. If you're familiar with the basic functions of the limbic system and stress response mechanism, you might like to skip or skim over some of Part 1.

Part 2: Boundaries in action is where the tyres hit the road and we explore the concept of boundaries in everyday situations that typically cause stress. We'll take the knowledge gained in Part 1, of how the brain responds to stimuli, and use this to look at how we become stressed by particular events (in relationships and friendships, at work, when attempting to find happiness, when we get angry) and how an understanding of boundaries can help reduce that stress. We also look at how and why we respond either rationally or emotionally to a situation. Finally, Part 2 concludes with some advice on positive ways to release the energy build-up that causes stress.

Before shining a new light on old concepts, adding a new perspective I believe could change your life, I want to make a few points so as not to be misunderstood.

The interaction between reason and emotion is the very nature of human development. However, I believe emotions and rational thinking are opposed to each other. A bit like Mr Spock on *Star Trek*. Using both emotions and reason in a balanced way is our ideal condition; and in order to help restore that lost balance, this book focuses on situations where this balance has been disturbed. To define this more clearly, we'll need to look at the original emotion: fear.

Over the millennia fear has expressed itself in ever more sophisticated ways and developed into the variety of emotions we experience and distinguish today, with some pretty sophisticated camouflage. I treat these as what they are at heart: simply different ways in which we express the original *fear of death* (or wish to survive) so that it becomes anger, aggression, sadness or any of the plethora of emotions we all experience differently and individually and yet, despite those differences, in a surprisingly similar way.

PART 1

The basic principles

1. **Boundaries**

When you strip away the physiological and psychological aspects of human behaviour to the bare essentials you arrive at a single, simple requirement: energy. Any action, be it physical (movement), spiritual, emotional or mental (neurons firing in the brain), is only possible if energy is available.

At its simplest, action is driven either by trying to preserve our life (looking for food) or avoid becoming food. Only when those needs are met do we then seek to maximize our pleasure. Our original emotion was fear — fear of starving or being eaten, which gives rise to the fight or flight response, or what I sometimes call the 'bash or dash' response. (We'll look at the neurological aspects of this in greater detail in Chapter 2 when we explore the limbic system.)

Over the millennia the fight or flight response has developed in increasingly sophisticated ways in regards to how we release this 'fear energy'. We don't necessarily 'bash' anymore, but may do so figuratively speaking — *throwing the book at someone* or *doing someone's head in*; or we might simply walk away from an argument as a 'dash' response.

We've grown accustomed to equating an action with an emotion: a person yells, so they must be angry. In turn, this interpretation of someone's action influences our future interactions with them.

We're now likely to act on what we perceive (in this case, that the person is angry) and make this perception the measuring stick, the defining principle against which all that follows is tested. What we experience as problems or difficulties are the result of the way this principle has become the driver of our interpretations, hopes and expectations.

Trying to untangle the different strands that add up to such a situation (what I call a 'tree-top' approach) is often as futile as trying to trace a single fibre of wool in a sweater. On the other hand, if you know the mechanism that led to the complication in the first place — the violation of a boundary or boundaries — there's no need for detailed analysis. Instead there is the instant relief of recognizing which boundaries have been crossed, and re-establishing their existence.

The more I work within the framework of boundaries and explain it to my clients, the more I'm reminded of breathing. We breathe so automatically and effortlessly we only become aware of its importance, and how many ways it can go wrong, when we have to gasp for air. In a similar way, when I outline the concept of boundaries, the reaction is sometimes underwhelming; it's so simple it's easily overlooked.

So what do I mean by boundaries? If we accept that I am *not* you and you're *not* me, then we accept there is a definite distinction between 'me' and 'you' and the rest of the world. Indeed, the idea of clear boundaries between one person and another, and one issue and another, certainly makes life a whole lot less complicated. While life is dominated by boundaries the challenge is to recognize, accept and stay within those boundaries.

This is no doubt an obvious and familiar concept. If you can say to yourself *I know this already*, then you're on the right track. The messages I've personally found to have a more lasting effect have been those that were almost familiar, rather than those requiring a leap of faith by leaving old thinking patterns behind and adopting new and unfamiliar ones. With this outlook and understanding of boundaries, we can distinguish between what is 'my problem' and what is 'your problem' without feeling guilty. This distinction is at the heart of boundary theory, and what I sometimes call a *boundary focus*.

Many of today's psychological interventions seem to involve tree-top analyses: attempts to explain or offer alternative ways to view situations, conditions and behaviours (also referred to as *presenting problems*). However, in an attempt to provide the answers, one difficult set of circumstances is often replaced with another.

I've found this approach a bit unhelpful when people who are already confused and feeling overwhelmed look for answers. This sort of analysis can make the solution seem even more complicated than the initial problem — and lead to new problems the searching soul may otherwise never have been aware of, without providing them with any relief or workable solutions.

Easing distress

When a client enters the room, I try to find something they can take away with them from their very first visit — something to help make their life a little easier, and preferably something that allows them to feel more comfortable with and within themselves.

On many occasions, understanding the brain activities underlying anxiety and depression provided encouragement — when clients saw for themselves that far from being 'terminal' these conditions are in fact simply functional. Instead of believing they were losing their minds they could see that their mind was only doing what it's designed to do. When a person fails to appreciate this fact, it can lead them to try to subdue their symptoms rather than remove the cause. This applies to all kinds of challenges in life, including interpersonal relationships at home or at work.

After more than twenty years (I'm a slow learner) I've come to realize that what makes us tick is based on just a few basic mechanisms, which explain what we're doing and why.

If you drive a Morris Minor or a Mercedes Benz, both will *only* transport you from point A to point B; they won't iron your shirt, make you dinner or pour you a drink. However, *how* you get from A to B may be quite a different experience, depending on which car you use. Likewise, while we're subject to basic principles that underlie and control our functioning, we've managed to throw in a few complications which make life a little less efficient, a little bit more interesting — and sometimes a lot more dramatic — than necessary.

I'm not saying either is better or worse. If your taste is for drama, so be it, and you can choose to design your life accordingly. Just as long as you did 'design' your life, rather than feeling as if you're living in a tumble dryer wondering who keeps pushing the button. And when people end up in a psychologist's office, it's usually the latter. The question you should be asking isn't *Is it wrong?* but rather *What's wrong?* or even more precisely, *What's not working for me?*

And since discomfort is the pre-condition for change, I ensure there isn't too much at work (which could prevent change), and just enough to facilitate it. A bit like Baby Bear's porridge — just right, according to Goldilocks.

Let's look at three cases I've seen at my practice, and then at a rather challenging question I often ask in response to stories such as these.

CASE STUDY 1: AARON

A middle-aged man presented to me complaining that his partner was making him 'feel guilty and miserable'. He could do nothing right and, worse still, whenever he thought he had done 'the right thing' she was quick to make him feel he had done something wrong, yet again!

CASE STUDY 2: ANNE AND PETER

A young couple came to see me, who appeared to be switched on and financially secure. Both were in well-paying positions and seemed (at face value anyway) to be the 'perfect' couple. They maintained eye contact when they talked about each other, even when they were complaining about the other person — yet she felt he was hiding things. He said he tried to be as honest as possible but sometimes failed to remember small details or thought they weren't important, although he admitted he tried to protect her sometimes by deliberately not telling her everything in order to avoid worrying her unnecessarily. She was very unhappy about this and felt betrayed to the point where she could no longer trust him. She complained he made her feel insecure and he said she made him feel guilty and inadequate, to the point where he was wondering if it was all worth it.

CASE STUDY 3: PAULINE

A middle-aged lady was looking for answers relating to her elderly mother, who made her life miserable. Whatever she did, her mother complained it was either unasked for, not enough or too much. She said her mother did all the talking, never listened, and never had a nice word to say about anybody. 'She makes me feel depressed' was her opening statement.

What do these case studies have in common? All these individuals shared the belief someone else had 'made' them do or feel something they didn't want to. You may agree that yes, people do *make* you feel in certain ways. My question to such statements is invariably: '*Make* you? How exactly do they do that? How do they *make* you . . .'

I suggest *no one* can make you feel, think or do anything. In the last example, how did the mother *make* her daughter do something? If I demand some action of you, I can do so by appealing to your good will, humanity, spiritual conviction — or whatever I think may do the trick, such as holding a gun to your head. The latter is often perceived as the ultimate persuader and, not surprisingly, also regarded as a convincing argument for being *made* to do something.

The fact is, ultimately *you* make the decision to succumb to my demand, request, persuasion or threat. Even with a gun thrown into the mix, despite the obvious risk, the final choice of whether to concede to a demand is yours to make. Think of the many martyrs throughout the course of history who willingly chose to die rather than succumb and give up their cause. Nobody *made* them decide on that course of action.

An uncertain outcome

Whatever the circumstances (even the most extreme), you're the only one with control over the choices you make in life. Whatever happens as a result of your decision, however, is beyond your control — and therein lies the problem. We don't like uncertainty; we like to know what *will* happen. Better still, we like to *determine* what will happen. But as the old joke says: *You want to make God laugh? Tell him your plans!*

It's this false belief — that *we* can determine how others will behave in the future as a result of *our* actions — which creates problems. In other words, we expect others to react the way we want them to or in the way we predicted, hoped or planned they would. When this expectation isn't fulfilled, we often blame either ourselves or the other person for it — and the groundwork for discontent is laid. Remember James, who gave his bemused partner some flowers in the introduction? In his case he neglected to focus on the real reason he wanted to buy flowers: his unexpressed expectation his partner would absolutely love the flowers (and James for buying them). In his mind she would have been so happy she would have showered him with affection.

As you can see, we can be very discerning when it comes to intentions and expectations. We tend to assume them in others, and depending on how we feel or our own expectation at the time, either appreciate them or pass judgment. When it comes to our own motives, however, we tend to ignore them or even deny their existence altogether. It may be a tad confronting to 'expose' yourself by admitting your effort was driven by an ulterior motive, which could be as simple as 'If she's happy, I'm happy'. The fact we may not be so economical with the truth deliberately is beside the point, and opinions about that may differ.

To summarize the point, and we'll get back to it a little later in more detail, nobody has the ability to 'make your day'. You simply *allow* someone to have that effect.

The 'God complex'

Can you *make* someone happy or unhappy? Can anyone *make you* happy or unhappy?

Whenever I ask this question most people say 'Yes, I can make my partner happy' or 'Yes, my partner can make me unhappy.' When I refer to my earlier examples and ask specifically *how* that happens, they soon realize their response was premature. Most people have difficulty specifying how they make someone else happy or unhappy or vice versa. When pressed to give me an example of something that makes them happy, most people soon realize some things make them happy some of the time, but nothing does the trick all the time — no matter the circumstances.

The answer seems to be 'it all depends'. If I'm in the right mood, then a particular treat, action or event can certainly make me happy. But whatever *makes* you happy would have to work anywhere, anytime and under any circumstance for it to be considered the recipe for happiness (or contentment, as I would prefer to call it). If it only makes you happy sometimes, often, or even most of the time, how would I know (when you're clearly unhappy) that today is the exception to the rule, and what worked previously isn't going to cut it?

The increasingly unavoidable conclusion seems to be that happiness doesn't depend on what *you* do for or to me, but how *I* feel at the time. You don't have the power to change my mood unless I'm willing or even able to let that happen. Sorry, you're not as omnipotent as you thought.

The overriding implication is that I'm responsible for my own feelings and you're responsible for yours. More generally, it doesn't depend on the intention of the giver, but on what the receiver thinks, feels, expects and is willing — and able — to accept.

Throughout this book, I will use simple diagrams to reinforce how complex concepts can be reduced to powerful symbols, thereby helping us to deconstruct difficult situations — in other words, creating visual boundaries that we can then apply to real situations. The two circles that you will meet on the next page symbolize the essence of 'boundaries'. Each circle represents not only a particular person or physical thing, but also any matter, issue or circumstance.

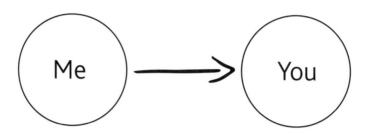

If you open yourself and let me in, you allow me to have an effect on you and I can *make* you happy. In reality, though, *you* decide to react any which way you want to — or think you have to react.

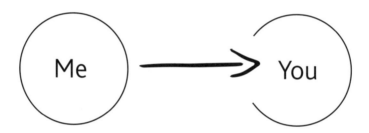

If, however, you don't allow my message to have any effect, it simply 'bounces off' into oblivion and there's nothing I can do about it. In this way, you've understood and respected the boundaries that separate me from you.

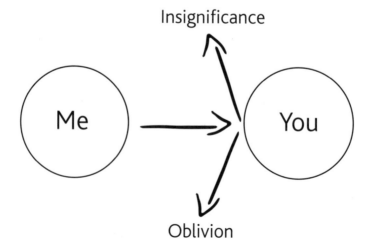

This is quite logical when you consider I can't make you physically do anything you don't want to do. Even if I held a gun to your head and you refused my request, all I could do would be to kill you — and you still wouldn't have done what I wanted. So how could I ever aspire to make you feel an emotion?

This is a very important point. The consequences of understanding and accepting this are profound, and like the tentacles of a jellyfish, reach into almost every aspect of human interaction. They are also at the root of the things we believe make our lives difficult and complicated.

If we believe someone makes us feel anything, it's because we allow it to happen. We each respond differently to what people do or say. If this were not the case, we would all respond in the same way to a particular event. We would all understand it the way it was meant to be taken rather than have our own interpretation. In fact the term *interpretation* wouldn't exist.

Reality, on the other hand, tells us we all have differing views on the same issue or event. Why else would we have various political parties, each reacting differently to the same piece of news, based on how it fits their own agenda?

We *only* have control over *our own actions*, not over how other people react. And sometimes our reaction may be totally unpredictable, surprising ourselves as well as everybody else. I'm pretty sure you would have experienced at least one occasion when you tried to do the right thing and acted with the best of intentions only to receive an unexpected reaction or rejection. Likewise, others only have control over their own actions, not over what you do or feel as a result of what they are or are not doing.

While all this may sound convincing, I can hear two unspoken questions and see your raised eyebrows: 'Are you saying I'm unable to make my partner happy? That the other person doesn't matter, and it's all just about me?'

Well, the answer is yes . . . and no. To what degree it's one or the other hopefully becomes clear as we move through the challenges this notion presents. At this point I merely wish to establish a bottom line, something we can agree on as a matter of fact rather than opinion.

The fact I can't make you feel anything isn't a matter of like or dislike. Much like the weather, it's a matter of fact; whether you like the weather is merely your opinion. This means that from now on, whenever you have a differing opinion or bothersome issue with someone, you can return to this unarguable bottom line against which you can test your differences. One of you will have violated the principle that you *can't* make anybody feel anything in particular — whatever they feel is ultimately their own choice, driven by their experiences, needs and whatever else influenced their reaction.

The implications of this are far reaching and may change the way you relate to people. While I categorically state that nothing and nobody can *make* us happy, I'm not implying particular people (or animals, events, things) don't have the capacity to enrich or diminish the quality of our experiences in life. They can and they do.

But while people can have an impact on our contentment, and the quality of it, they can never create it.

Just to clarify, I'm not talking about influence. Every time we engage in a conversation or say something funny or sad, we expect the other person to laugh or cry with us. In other words, we expect them to agree with our perspective of the story. But try as we may, ultimately our attempt to influence someone can only be successful if the other person allows it to happen. Otherwise there would be no such thing as a misfired joke or misunderstood intentions.

Some people can push your buttons — they may even do so on

purpose. For instance, the child who knows that if they keep pushing, their parents will eventually relent and give them what they want. Or the partner who knows that bringing up a particular issue will make the other feel guilty and not pursue a particular line of questioning, which allows them to get away with their opinion or bothersome behaviour.

Imagine if the buttons were no longer connected? Power failure, connection lost — what then? No matter how hard someone tried to push your buttons, nothing would happen. Your buttons would no longer be switched on. In other words, they would fail to get the response they expected. Just remember this — you're the only person who can disconnect your buttons.

So, let's make it official and say goodbye to our God complex. We can't make someone else feel any particular emotion. While we can try to manipulate or influence other people, we can't control the outcome. What's even more liberating is the notion that *we don't have to.*

The first lesson in life

To begin to understand the concept of boundaries and what this all means, we must first understand the most important question of all — who am I?

When a baby is born, psychoanalytical theory (courtesy of Mr Freud and friends) contends that the baby regards its mother's breasts as part of itself. In other words, the baby hasn't yet differentiated between itself and its mother. Given that, at birth, the only thing the baby knows is itself — having had no other reference point in the womb — it's a reasonable proposition that the baby comes into the world with the intrinsic, albeit unconscious assumption of being at one with the world. (Incidentally, this is an interesting idea from many spiritual viewpoints; that we'll eventually return to this stage after death, becoming one with the 'universe' or God or whatever name, shape, concept or form you believe the afterlife may take.)

This concept also makes sense from a neurological point of view, as there is physiological support for this contention. For instance, we know the visual acuity of newborns is only about 8 inches or 20 centimetres, beyond which everything else is blurry. Now take a guess at the distance from a mother's eyes to baby's eyes when she cradles it in her arms. You got it: about 20 centimetres.

For a baby, learning about boundaries starts with *who's who in the zoo*. Lesson one: I am different from Mum. Lesson two: Mum and Dad are different from each other, and so on. Each person is determined by their voice, smell, feel, shape and size — in other words, their *boundaries*. This is how we determine and distinguish one person or thing from another.

A country is only recognized as being separate from its neighbours when its physical boundaries are clearly defined. Similarly, many religions are defined by their different beliefs and values. Think of how many wars have broken out as a result of physical boundaries being transgressed or the perception of religious boundaries not being respected. Boundaries underlie and define our perceptions and the way we understand and organize the world. Quite simple, isn't it? And yet we use confusion, ignorance, and whatever else the human mind can come up with, as an excuse for transgressing and abusing boundaries, which in turn creates many of the problems we find so difficult to solve. On the other hand, it's easy to see how this happens since even well-defined boundaries aren't always clear to others or set in stone.

Which of the following do you consider to be your immediate family? Is it the one you started yourself (your partner and your children) or the one you were raised in (your parents and siblings)?

Often the answer to this question only becomes relevant when interests and expectations clash and an important family decision must be made. Then division can run straight through what had previously been thought of as a clearly defined unit.

The distinction of boundaries not only applies to physical entities, but also to personal 'space' (in the literal sense and also in terms of the freedom to be ourselves). In a physical sense, where does your 'space' start and end? Is there a rule or is it simply defined by our own personal definition of what 'my space' is?

Several studies on personal space have shown that the distance individuals consider to be their personal space differs significantly between cultures. In Europe it increases the further north people live — for example, Swedes tend to stand further apart when talking to each other than Italians. Similar findings are recorded for North Americans and those from South America. Not appreciating these differences can obviously lead to severe misunderstandings, whether a person is considered rude for keeping their distance or intrusive for seeking closeness.

Most of us need to maintain a certain distance from another person (unless they are very familiar to us) to feel comfortable with them. Too close and we feel uncomfortable, too far and we remain strangers.

Predictability

Psychology was challenged to explain human behaviour in the wake of World War II and the atrocities that accompanied the Nazi regime. Indeed, it appeared to struggle for direction. Abraham Maslow's hierarchy of needs was an almost back to basics approach, claiming that before we can aspire to strive for the 'greater good' and other ideals, we must first have our basic needs (water, food, safety and shelter) met.

For me, Mr Maslow overlooked the need for boundaries as one

of humanity's most basic needs. It's directly related to the need for predictability, which as we shall see shortly, is a predictor of stress.

Boundaries provide a roadmap for some, while for others they offer a way of climbing even higher up the tree mentioned earlier, discovering increasingly more about themselves and the world around them.

Ultimately, though, boundary focus isn't the answer — it simply points the way to finding a solution. Let me explain why, by introducing what I consider to be an underrated basic human need.

Imagine you're at a crowded beach on a lazy sunny afternoon. To escape the noise, you decide to lie down in a small dinghy anchored just offshore. You close your eyes and before you know it, you're fast asleep. Upon opening your eyes you notice nothing but water all around you. The realization suddenly hits you: the dinghy has broken free. You have no concept of where the beach is or even how far out to sea you've drifted. What would be the most frightening aspect of this situation for you?

Would it be realizing you're lost at sea? Of course it would! What would you do to get out of the situation? Start rowing would be the obvious answer. OK — in which direction? Hmm, good question. So wouldn't the *most* frightening aspect actually be not knowing where you are in relation to land and safety?

From the stories of survivors of such situations, we know that once a sense of direction is established, a person feels a sense of hope and comfort and is more prepared to try, even knowing there may still be formidable obstacles to overcome. In other words, even if we know we may not make it to safety, we'll die trying if we have some indication of where safety lies.

Now, if you found some water and food reserves in the dinghy, would that relieve your anxiety? I venture to suggest you wouldn't throw them overboard, but at the same time, they would only prevent you from starving or dying of thirst. It wouldn't alleviate your fear about your situation and the fact you could die. And, if you had the choice between hunting for food as a school of fish swim past and making yourself known to a passing ship, which option would you take?

This serves to differentiate our need for food and water from our much deeper-seated need for predictability and a sense of control over our fate. It seems to indicate that in addition to the basic human needs outlined by Maslow there is another equally basic need that tends to slip under the radar. Predictability or, more specifically, the lack of it.

Much like predictability, boundaries describe and contain. They allow us to distinguish one thing or person from another. Lack of predictability is the flipside of the coin and the reason why the crossing of boundaries is at the heart of so many of life's problems.

When we mix metaphors they stop making sense. When we mix substances — another violation of boundaries — we do so at our peril. Adding water to wine may allow you to drink more or may get you fined for fraud. However, mixing a highly caustic substance with a highly combustible and explosive substance creates the most valuable asset on this planet: water (the result of hydrogen mixed with oxygen). Boundaries provide predictability and consistency. Their violation, on the other hand, results in unpredictable situations that are sometimes dangerous while at other times life saving.

In humans, unpredictability or a violation of boundaries often triggers a stress reaction. Imagine how you would feel if you never knew for sure whether you would get paid at the end of each month. Or if a stranger knocked on your door to introduce himself as your new tenant (with a piece of paper in his hand to prove it) because the law had been changed overnight. An unpredictable situation can be extremely unsettling.

The problem lies in the fact that we often fail to recognize when we're guilty of violating boundaries because they come in all different shapes, sizes and contexts. Often they bear different names and we don't even recognize them as boundaries. We may call them *situations, opinions, attitudes* and so on. Unfortunately, applying different labels only adds to the confusion.

Understanding boundaries in a very broad sense creates a paradigm shift, as it allows us to see the world differently and more simply. Consider a map that includes every road from major highways to narrow country lanes in a densely populated area. The map is likely to look very crowded and could prove useless to someone unfamiliar with the area. Finding their way would be like navigating through a maze. Now imagine another map with only major arterial roads highlighted. This map would be useless if you were looking for a particular address, but helpful if you merely wanted to get an idea about the general direction you have to travel.

In a similar way, the idea of boundaries lets you recognize overarching rules lost through too many complex differentiations. As a result, we've become used to seeing and treating each issue or problem situation as being subject to different rules.

Boundaries aren't only a guiding principle, they also come with inherent rules. The benefit here is that they aren't subject to debate. The rules are contained by their defining boundaries. A car is a car. Treating the car as something that simply moves people or objects from A to B allows me to attend to other important issues, such as building roads and establishing road rules. Violation of these boundaries can lead to the logically impoverished view, for example, that *speed kills*. While it's a factor in road fatalities, it doesn't *cause* them. Poor road conditions, driver error, misjudgment and other human shortcomings — of which one could be misjudging the speed the driver can handle — cause accidents. Focusing simply on speed as a cause leads to ineffective speed restrictions while people still die in car accidents.

While not a cure-all, the concept of boundaries can help define and thereby contain a problem. Rather than getting rid of cars because of a mistaken belief that people can have accidents in them if they fail to adhere to the road rules, boundaries allow us to deal with each aspect (car safety versus nature of accidents) separately and find a solution for each.

Liberated by boundaries — how so?

Regardless of what anybody does, your own perception, mood or inclination will determine how you respond to their actions. Something that may please at one time may be very annoying under different circumstances. Think of something quite pleasant, let's say a tickle. Now imagine it continuing for half an hour and the tickle soon turns into an annoying itch. Same tickle, same tickler, same you, but a different reaction.

Just as this example shows no person can make us happy, if we look closely we can also see that in fact nothing external to ourselves can do the trick either. As sobering as this realization may be, it's also liberating as it removes the unrealistic expectation of being responsible for your partner's happiness. Sure, you may do things they find nice, considerate or 'lovely', and as a result they might decide you made them happy. But there's no guarantee.

Let's move on to another example. How about an old favourite, money? If I had more money, I'd be so happy! Sound familiar?

Reality: if you're already a happy chappie and win $1 million, you'll be a happy chappie with $1 million. If you're miserable and win $1 million you'll simply be miserable with $1 million. Even if you're momentarily happy, being miserably inclined you'll find something wrong with your good fortune: the winner the previous week won $10 million; or it took two weeks before you had the money in your account; or you'll moan about all that extra tax you'll have to pay on any earnings from your win. See what I mean? Just winning the money won't suddenly make you happy.

If not money, what about friends? No question they can enrich your life and make it interesting, and lighten the load. But can they make you feel something in particular? Again, it depends on how you perceive what they're doing . . . and your expectations. There's no guarantee that what they do will have the desired effect *on you*. If friends could make you feel good, there would be no such thing as a fall-out between friends; being friends they would *always* keep you happy.

If these things can't make you happy, what else is there? True love. That's got to be it. 'You've made me so very happy' . . . but here comes another bubble-buster. What I'm really saying is that you've got what it takes to tickle my fancy and I'm happy you grant me that benefit. It doesn't really make a practical difference how we phrase the fact that I love you and enjoy your company. As so often is the case, the difference lies in the detail and only becomes apparent when things go south. Then the mistaken belief that 'you've made me happy' can lead to the accusation I now 'made you' unhappy and I'm held responsible for something that was always beyond my control. The more you tell yourself that I'm the one who made you happy, the more desperate you'll become, because in your mind I'm now the 'only one' who can make you happy again. Don't get me wrong — true love is great, as long as you don't treat it as something that 'makes' you happy.

Let's hope I've broken it to you gently. There is no external object or person capable of *making* us feel anything. It will *always* be our disposition that decides what emotion a particular action or event provokes within us. No exceptions.

Internalising an external event

When we experience discomfort, the feeling is usually associated with a specific event that crosses our path or interferes with our plans. Or we may worry about someone we care about. We may fear a confrontation, or some other unpleasant event that might occur. In each case we're reacting to something that is external to ourselves with what we've come to call an emotion.

Simplified it looks like this. There is you, and then there is an external *thing*, which could be another person, a relationship, an issue or problem.

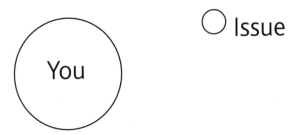

The problem remains detached from me. We then deal with the problem and accept the outcome. We may not like it, but because we respect the boundary between ourselves and the (external) issue, we simply get on with life.

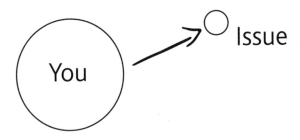

However, we often mistakenly internalize the external event, problem or person, which then becomes a part of us. In our misguided belief that something external can make us feel good — and we give it the power to do so — it follows that only that same *something* has the power to make us feel the opposite.

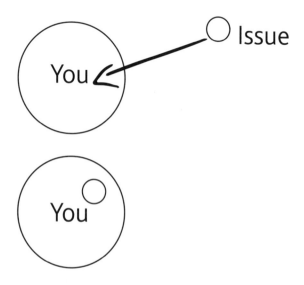

If someone did make us feel good, what if they change their mind; if a thing, what if we lose it? If a person made us feel bad, when will they make us feel better again? We have no way of knowing if or when it will occur, and no control over it. A very stressful situation indeed.

After all, it's a matter of circumstance — and circumstances change. We can't universally claim a particular event would make us feel anything. While certain reactions are likely, they are by no means guaranteed. It's not the event; it's our disposition *at the time of the event* that determines how we'll respond. In other words, it's nothing outside of us, but our own, internal disposition.

This schematic representation is probably at the root of many of our troubles, if not most of them. When we choose to make something our problem it may indeed turn out to become just that: our problem. This includes accepting that someone else's reaction or feeling is *our* responsibility. Following an argument, the statement 'You made me feel miserable' may provoke a sense of guilt. This powerful feeling could lead you to assume responsibility for 'making' that person unhappy. But be warned: once you take that mental step, there's basically no way of going back. You're the one holding the baby now. I can pull that string and make you feel guilty again and again at my leisure, because you've accepted that you made me unhappy.

When we accept someone else's problem as our own, without maintaining and respecting their right to their problem, we all but assume ownership of it, effectively emasculating the other person. What we're really saying is: *You're unable to look after yourself and resolve the situation, so I have to do it for you.* Would we want to be told that ourselves?

Instead of leaving it where it belongs we load ourselves up with a problem we can't possibly resolve — because it's not ours to solve. What we may see as a solution isn't necessarily accepted or acceptable to the other person.

As a result we experience stress, be it over our own perceived inability to solve a problem or the other person's perceived stubbornness not to accept what we see as the obvious solution, completely disregarding the fact that it's only 'obvious' to us. We become anxious, depressed, stressed or otherwise indisposed or miserable and have to consult a professional to help us out of the mess we got ourselves into, simply by not respecting our boundaries. We've waded in, extended ourselves to encompass the problem and then found we can't solve it. Once you internalize something and make it yours the seed for stress has been sown.

Why? Because you've now incorporated something 'foreign' into yourself, and while you can try to influence or manipulate events to a particular end, you have no control over the outcome. The best you can hope for is that your endeavours work out. But as the circles in the figures so far have shown, instead of respecting that a problem has its own existence and boundary, you have internalized something over which you have no control, and can't predict how it will end. As a result you feel stressed.

The reason why this internalizing causes us to feel stressed takes us a little deeper into what ultimately makes us tick as humans. What happens when I feel 'stressed right out of my brain' as the saying goes?

To find out, let's consider the brain a little closer, so we can start to appreciate the mechanisms involved when we breach boundaries, internalize what's outside ourselves and become stressed.

2. **Stress**

Stress! It almost seems to be the modern equivalent of having a slave: everyone should have one. You almost can't do without it; in fact, it seems prerequisite for joining the in-crowd and being able to contribute to the conversation about gloriously stressful stress. Some folks seem to thrive on it — but what exactly is it?

To understand why stress is a fundamental response hardwired into our brain I have to take you back to its origin, which is necessary to make the connection between boundaries — and their violations — stress and emotions. First we need to clarify what stress and emotion mean in physiological, neurological and psychological terms. Let's have a look at the brain and its place in the hierarchy. How to manage what we experience as 'stress' will be discussed in Part 2.

Now don't worry — this isn't a detailed scientific analysis of brain functions and processes — instead I'll try to give you a simple overview of how the brain has evolved, the practical implications for the concept of boundaries and why the consequences can be so dramatic when they're violated. I'll also try to explain how stress and emotion impact our daily functioning, so some finer details will be neglected in favour of the bigger picture. While you won't turn into a brain surgeon, I'll consider my mission accomplished if you finish reading with a better understanding of the concept of 'control' and the importance of 'predictability' in the context of boundaries.

Remember tree-top analysis? Well now I want to apply the analogy to the brain. This is fitting from two angles: the brain developed 'upwards' like a growing plant; and this familiar comparison can also help us understand its workings. So we can either start at the tree-top and work our way down, at the risk of getting lost in its complexity, or start from the ground level and follow it upwards. I've chosen the latter, so I can stop climbing any time things become too complicated. At that point I can then decide if my thirst or need for knowledge has been quenched or if I want to delve further into the matter to reach a deeper level of understanding.

When you understand what happens in the brain just before you react to anything someone says or does, you can take control over those reactions and avoid the almost instinctual responses, which often give rise to consternation and frustration — and contribute to what we then experience as a 'problem'. To appreciate the true role of stress as a survival mechanism, which is activated on a daily basis — particularly in our interpersonal relationships — we need to go back in time.

Why do we have a brain?

Life started with simple one-cell organisms, happily swimming around in the ocean minding their own business. So why did they start to develop a structure that's now the most complex in the known universe, with more neural connections in a single human brain than stars in our galaxy?

There's a range of possible answers: to complete the daily cryptic crossword challenge, become a chess champion, excel at crochet or fly to the moon. Or could it simply be to increase the chance of survival?

In 1990 the neurologist Paul MacLean proposed the triune brain theory and suggested the brain's functions developed from the bottom up. In the process, the area we now know as the brain stem became increasingly sophisticated. Each new skill, reflected in the brain building new neural connections, gave the animal a better chance to live longer and procreate to its heart's content.

To gain a very simple representation of the human brain, make a fist with both hands, holding them together at the thumbs, which are enclosed. Your wrists would represent the brain stem, the most primitive part of the brain, also known as the *reptilian brain*. Since reptiles are the last survivors of the dinosaur era, the name also indicates it's a very early stage of brain development. At that stage it would probably be true to say that not much was going on between the ears. The brain stem regulates the essential functions of the body such as heart rate, breathing and body temperature, balance, as well as the first reflexes of what has become known as the 'fight or flight' response.

At the next stage the *paleomammalian complex* developed, represented by your thumbs in our hand-fist model of the brain. MacLean called this the *limbic system*. The number of its components and variety of its functions have recently led to suggestions that it acts as a relay station between incoming stimuli and our emotional responses. The limbic system is involved in evaluating stimuli, for example letting us know if something is dangerous or pleasant, triggering and differentiating emotional responses based on the individual's range of experiences as well as the formation of memory.

The latter may seem strange, since memory is normally associated with different parts of the *neocortex*, the upper and most advanced section of the brain. However, how would we know something is dangerous if the information wasn't based on our experiences, which we store as memories? It makes a lot of sense that, although still quite primitive, the limbic system stores information, which at a later stage is integrated into our long-term memory. In the beginning it probably only enabled us to avoid life-threatening situations, before becoming one of the features making humans distinct from other mammals: our sense of history — our own, that of others, or of a series of events and our place in them.

The limbic system was quite an advance on the basic function of the reptilian brain. It allowed the organism to detect danger, and helped it to decide if something represented a potential threat to its survival. If the faint sound it detected was just leaves rustling in the wind it could go back to whatever it was doing. However, if the sound was from a potential predator or an unexplained 'novelty', the limbic system would kick-start the body into action, preparing the organism to either fight or run for safety. This is the fight or flight response, which is still the main driving force when we get ourselves into gear. Later the limbic system also helped refine our basic affects (I use the term in its psychological meaning of emotional response, or how we react to stimuli), resulting in the richness and diversity of what we now call emotions.

During the last stage of brain development, the *neomammalian complex*, the neocortex evolved into what we now associate with the thinking brain, allowing us to construct abstract thoughts, think in numbers and carry out sequential planning. It also provides us with the structures that give us speech. In our hand model the neocortex would correspond to the back of the hand, the knuckles and the fingers enclosing the thumbs.

The triune theory of the brain isn't universally accepted; however, despite some valid questions being raised, the evidence for triune theory seems stronger than the objections. These questions only seem to lend support to concepts already accepted: that evolution didn't occur in a straight line. It seems not only logical that the brain developed in stages, but there is also ample supporting evidence when comparing the mental capabilities of creatures at different stages along the evolutionary ladder.

The concept underlying the triune brain provides a very useful background to appreciate what we call 'anxiety' and 'depression' as normal processes, challenging the concept of them both as disorders. I prefer to see them as the brain doing exactly what it's supposed to do: sending messages, which we unfortunately often fail to decipher properly. But we'll look at this in more detail later on.

Two halves

There's a further aspect of brain development we need to talk about, which is essential in the context of stress and emotions and how they are linked to boundaries.

On its developmental journey from the bottom (brain stem) to the top (neocortex), the brain split into two halves at some stage, when things started to appear in twos. Two arms, legs and eyes. The eyes, however, presented a problem. Due to their distance from each other, each eye projects its own image onto the retina. We would therefore perceive two slightly different images if it wasn't for a very clever structure within our brain known as the *optic chiasm*. This enables stereoscopic vision, which combines the different input from each eye into the single picture the brain ultimately registers. It also means each half of the brain controls the opposite side of the body. Originally this didn't have any functional significance, but things changed when we started to use implements to manipulate our environment — poking around with sticks, spear fishing or throwing stones for defence and hunting.

Some theories suggest that when we developed a preference for using the right hand to do most things, the left brain half was stimulated to develop new structures to coordinate the right hand, ultimately leading to a functional division of labour between the two halves of the brain. With these new skills our mental sophistication increased, extended to making plans and we became future directed, able to handle abstract concepts and symbolic representations.

And most importantly, we started to communicate our intentions verbally. Since the production of language developed much later than our tendency to bash an aggressor's head in when we had to defend ourselves, the ability to put thoughts into words is predominantly also reserved for the left brain and is why your language centre is located in your left brain hemisphere.

This side is now the one that processes mental tasks, and is responsible for what we call thinking or cognition, while the right-hand side has retained its responsibility for ensuring survival — and specializes in the processing of emotions.

Many questions about brain development are still debated, and the concept of a strict separation between right and left-hand brain isn't universally accepted. Indeed, as much as there is evidence for certain abilities being associated with a particular side of the brain, we need to acknowledge a number of inconsistencies, which throw up some questions about a strict right/left division of the brain.

In more than 90 percent of right-handed people, speech production occurs in the left hemisphere, but in 50 percent of left-handers it's either bi-lateral or more prominent in the right hemisphere. This cements the fact there is a rule and deviations from it.

*It's because **we know how the brain normally** **works that we can appreciate the exceptions** **from its default setting.***

One may treat certain occurrences as exceptions to the rule, but it may also be seen as the result of a discovery that, while hardly new, is still underappreciated: the plasticity of the brain.

Plasticity of the brain — how to shape your future

For a long time we believed the structures in the brain were fixed and our different abilities — such as hearing, speech, bodily movements, etc. — were unalterably assigned to a particular area. However, people who had suffered a stroke affecting their speech centre in their left brain could recover their speech, and children with damage to particular areas of their brains were able to compensate by activating other parts, which then took over the function of the damaged or compromised area. These observations led to a rethink and the idea of a malleable, or plastic, brain — known as neuroplasticity — is now generally accepted. In this case, plastic doesn't mean something cheap you can buy from the thrift shop; instead, it uses the original meaning of the term.

Sometimes other areas do take over enabling brain functions that seemed lost, such as speech. In other cases, for example blindness, it may result in the remaining senses being sharpened to compensate for the visual defect, resulting in a heightened perception that can be almost as effective as visual perception or in some cases even outperform those with eyesight.

Neuroplasticity also provides us with opportunities to create our own future. In more colloquial terms it means you *can* teach an old dog new tricks. Research has demonstrated that, in simple terms, the brain remains plastic into old age, able to form new neural connections or connect existing structures in novel ways. In fact, this happens every time our brain is exposed to a new experience.

Every time we learn a new skill, are surprised and then adjust our responses accordingly, with every experience that causes us to rethink what we thought we knew and reconsider the consequences this may have, neural pathways either connect in new ways or form new connections.

On the other hand we may often feel as trapped in a cycle of endlessly repeating old experiences and unpleasant memories, seemingly unable to let them go. We end up feeling depressed, anxious, angry or guilty all over again.

To understand this process, consider that with every reiteration these memories become stronger, keeping us captive in the cycle of unpleasant memories for longer. The more often we remember, the stronger the memory becomes. It's the essence of memory that the more we go over the same event, the less likely we are to forget it. In a different context we call this process 'learning'. Unfortunately, this goes for unwelcome as much as for welcome memories. In extreme cases we call it post-traumatic stress — memories are reiterated rather than processed and integrated into the long-term memory system as a singular event and no longer a persistent threat.

The more we think outside our own square and are open to new experiences we contribute to the process of 'unlearning' old information. New thoughts and impressions require the brain to create new neural pathways. By definition 'new' means the brain has to encode information differently, or bring old information into a different, unfamiliar context. The brain has to change with every new experience otherwise it wouldn't be experienced as 'new' and instead would be referred to as 'memory'.

While we may not be able to control the electric energy or the influence of chemicals that enable the brain to do its job, it's important to stress they only activate *existing* networks. They allow access to what's already stored as a memory, the thoughts and ideas based on this information and encoded in these neural structures. Changing our brain means encouraging it to lay down new pathways, allowing these to form new connections and linking differently to existing ones — in effect, creating complete new networks.

Forging new pathways

Contrary to the understanding that brain functions are the result of electric potentiation and chemical activity, chemicals and electrical impulses only enable the neural networks we call 'the brain' to function; they are the fuel allowing the engine to run. To alter the way the brain functions more effectively, it's not enough to interfere in the chemical interplay; as we have discussed before, it requires changing the neural networks and the way they're connected.

As these new pathways are established, instead of reiterating old 'memories', and strengthening well-exercised thought patterns, the old pathways wither — the process we know as forgetting — and we take another step in shaping our future. The answer to helping the brain change seems a rather simple one. All we need to do is provide it with new challenges and feed it new information — preferably information we'd like to remember. One way we can start this change is by doing familiar activities in unfamiliar ways, such as using your other hand to brush your teeth or peel an apple. (Better keep a band-aid ready. But you improve with practice, as your brain changes.)

Isn't it practice that makes perfect? Yes. The more you do something the better you get at it. However, just like *use it or lose it*, another principle of brain functionality, *practice makes perfect* is simply an observation, not an explanation. The *explanation* is that neural pathways are strengthened when the axons of connecting cells become myelinated, and electric impulses are transmitted faster, resulting in quicker processing of information and faster reaction times. Our brain is changing — we've learned a new skill and are *getting better* at it.

The obvious downside to the brain's plasticity is the way we use it. While we can lay down desirable new pathways and patterns, the brain doesn't really discern between what we regard as good or bad, or as I prefer to call it, helpful or unhelpful. Yes, we can acquire new habits, but they may be quite destructive. Unfortunately, practice makes perfect also applies to thinking unhelpful thoughts. Addictions of any kind are another example of how the brain changes because of the way we teach it, in this case not to our advantage. The development of anxiety and phobias is another example of how practising unhelpful behaviour patterns can lead to changes in the brain.

It's also worth considering that while the brain influences the way we do things, the way we conduct ourselves in response changes the way the brain functions. It's a two-way street. We manipulate our environment through our thought processes, and the environment has its reciprocal influence on the way we think, by giving us cues about what we're trying to avoid or achieve. The goals we set for ourselves are shaped by what's around us, as much as it influences how realistic and achievable we see our goals as being.

This raises the philosophical point about our *perfectibility*, our ability to change and improve ourselves, going all the way back to the Greek philosopher Aristotle. Of course, the question arises: What does *improvement*, or *ideal development* entail? This is strongly linked to the question *to what end?* In my opinion Mr Maslow, referred to earlier, provided the answer. While he may have not included boundaries in his hierarchy of needs, he postulated *self-actualization* as the ultimate goal in human development. Since it refers to the 'self', it also avoids a definition of what one 'should' attain or may be universally seen as desirable, and leaves the answer with each individual.

Before I conclude this chapter I'll leave you with a clarifying remark. The brevity of the way I've dealt with brain-plasticity, or neuroplasticity as it's also known, is inversely related to its relevance in neuropsychology and psychological interventions. Boundary-focused therapy, for example, is not only influenced by, but makes extensive use of, neuroplasticity, which is also at the heart of how we now understand the brain and its operation. In fact, a challenge to conventional treatments of so-called 'disorders' is already taking place in the form of what currently goes under the name *neuropsychotherapy*.

The benefits of an enriched environment from birth and when practising new skills later in life have been shown to increase the volume and thickness of the brain. It can change our 'brain maps' and exponentially increase the number of neural connections. These findings will increasingly affect the way therapy is conducted as much as it will change the way we use — or stop using — chemical interventions (psychoactive medication) when it comes to treating depression and anxiety. In this regard the future can't come fast enough.

3. **Fear, the ultimate driving force**

We've now explored a little about how the brain developed and how its structures are laid down. Having identified the structures, however, doesn't tell us the process, the way in which this 'hardware' could be used most effectively.

The sensation of 'fear' seems to have achieved just that. It was fear that alerted the organism to impending danger, to the possibility of being hurt, eaten or driven out of familiar territory.

Fear, then, deserves the rank of the original 'emotion', and every other emotion can be linked back to it. For example, fear of death or physical harm manifests as aggression or defensive behaviour, while fear that one's gene pool won't survive is experienced as jealousy or revenge. Fear of death is the overriding driving force. When activated it results in the first instance in 'unreflected' actions, and at its most instinctual, the fight or flight response, which we could well exchange for the much more familiar term *stress*.

Still running after all those years

What happens in the brain just before we decide to run or fight? For the answer to this we need to go back a few hundred thousand years, because not much has changed in the meantime.

Consider the following scenario. You stumble through the wilderness in search of food, and follow a trail, which you think may lead to culinary reward, when you hear a sound behind you. It could be something innocent, like the wind, or it could mean you're being hunted. Your brain, or the limbic system to be more precise, plays it safe and assumes the latter, making sure you have the best chance of getting out of a potentially terminal situation.

When you turn around to face the potential danger, no matter if you decide to run away or fight, you need energy, and your limbic system throws everything at the situation it possibly can to stay alive. It's here that the efficiency of your limbic system comes into play. Within the limbic system your thalamus gains input while your amygdala rapidly tries to figure out what it could mean. If it decides the sound indicates something potentially dangerous, or recognizes it as a known threat, it sends a signal to the hypothalamus. This in turn sends a signal down the line that sets off a number of reactions in your body.

It activates your adrenal glands, which release a number of different 'stress hormones' of which adrenaline and cortisol are probably the most commonly known. The physical mechanisms we need most to stay alive are powered up, while those we don't have a particular need for, or that are useless in this situation, are deactivated.

What we do need, and in great quantity, is oxygen, which gives us endurance. Just as important as the need for oxygen at this time is our need for glucose (sugar), which provides the 'fuel' or the energy for the engine that is our body, in particular for our muscles, which will execute our actions. Oxygen and glucose allow the muscles to do their job.

To ensure there's as much oxygen available as possible, in response to the additional stress hormones now circulating in the system, we change the way we breathe. While we normally breathe in oxygen, part of which is converted into carbon dioxide and exhaled, we now want to hang on to the oxygen (it's energy, after all) and start breathing rapidly, in effect pumping ourselves up as athletes do before a sprint. We also do this every time we want to lift something heavy and count to 'three', in the meantime pumping air into our lungs, then releasing the energy in one explosive action when the object is lifted. By breathing quickly, the body has less time to convert the oxygen into carbon dioxide, instead it is retained as oxygen, sent it to our muscles and we have more energy available.

The air we breathe out still consists of oxygen as well as carbon dioxide, but the percentage of each has changed, and that makes all the difference: too much CO_2 and you're dead; not enough and you're also dead. Life or death is determined by a delicate balance between the two. And while it's a very important one, it's only one aspect of what happens in your body when stress hormones are released, but it's sufficient to trigger the physiological changes we then notice.

In order to be able to run away or fight we need oxygen in the muscles in our arms and legs. As they're furthest from the heart, blood pressure is now increased to get the oxygen to them. The heart rate also increases, because we want as much of the good stuff as fast as possible. The more oxygen the system is able to provide, the longer we can sustain our physical efforts. Your brain, more precisely the amygdala via a 'feedback loop', notices the presence of the stress hormone cortisol and concludes we're still under attack and keeps initiating the release of more stress hormones, making more oxygen available to ensure we can keep running or fighting for our life, setting up a self-feeding cycle.

Survival is now your main focus and while making energy available, your body also begins to conserve energy where it can. Any activity that's not absolutely essential is stopped or reduced. Among the first is the awareness of pain. While we're in the process of defending ourselves any pain signals would only distract our attention from the aggressor, and likely result in more pain and subsequent defeat as the attacker takes advantage of our distraction. The pain sensors in your skin are shut down, and only return to action when the fight is over and we can afford to attend to the damage we sustained, as animals do when they lick their wounds after a fight.

When subjected to a stressful event we often also find we can't eat or our appetite disappears. Instead we experience nausea or a sensation similar to having 'rocks in the stomach' — it seems impossible to eat and some people may even throw up as a result of a stressful experience.

One of the reasons for this is simply that when we're fighting or running for survival, digesting food sucks up energy when we need it much more urgently in our muscles. We need the 'fuel' (glucose) now and we have no time to wait until undigested food is processed and converted into usable energy. The digestive system is shut down and blood supply to the stomach restricted, resulting in the familiar 'knot'.

Rather than receiving fuel from the stomach, the organism turns to other areas in the body where sugar is deposited as an emergency supply, such as the liver. Stored as glycogen, it's now converted back into glucose and sent to the muscles, where together with oxygen we now have a useable energy source and are ready to let loose.

This is what happens when under threat of attack, until we know we're safe. For those unable to out-run or overpower their attacker, the story ends right here. But what about the survivors — how does their system know the threat has passed and it's time to stop releasing stress hormones?

The wind-down phase — our salvation

Having avoided ending up as someone else's food, the aim is to stay that way and find a safe place where we can rest and recover. When the body is in rest mode breathing slows, and we breathe into the diaphragm instead of the chest, reducing the oxygen content in our blood, because we only need minimal energy now — just enough to allow the vital functions to operate.

Since you only breathe that way when you rest, and you only rest when safe, this is the signal to the brain to stop the release of stress (activation) hormones; it's as simple as that. If you want to observe how it works have a look at a sleeping baby, as its tummy gently rises and falls in blissful sleep. When we're asleep, we breathe the same way.

To summarize, when you detect a threat (real or potential) your body prepares to defend itself and releases stress hormones. Once the threat has passed and we rest ('catch our breath'), the brain issues the signal to cease the release of stress hormones and the body returns to normal functioning.

This activation sequence is a short-term response by the body to an impending threat. The emphasis here is on *short-term*. If this response pattern is prolonged the effect on the whole system turns from functional to taxing and eventually damaging — just like revving up a car engine and keeping it in the red zone of the tachometer for an extended period of time. Since the wear on the engine is considerably more than running it within the normal range of operation, it's likely to break down well before its calculated potential.

The causes of stress

You might have noticed I used words like *stress* and *stressful* when describing the effects of fear on the body. In fact, stress sits between fear and emotions, somehow connecting the two.

This might seem somewhat contradictory; however, it reflects the evolutionary process of emotions. Fear initiates the physiological changes we call stress, and the energy this produces is released in what we now experience as different emotions.

Before we make that connection, though, let me tell you about a discovery that not only allows us to identify what stress is, but also provides the link between the primeval process of the fight or flight response to a threat to our boundaries.

The inter-connectedness of the physiological and emotional reactions makes matters complicated. Stress drives our almost automatic reaction of assigning an emotional value to an event that by itself is *value neutral*. As a consequence, it's then seen as threatening or endearing or everything in between, which is the very nature of human relationships. So, what is this mechanism called stress that's at the root of our personal and interpersonal problems?

In 1968 a young Dr Weiss, a professor at Yale University having just attained his PhD, published an article 'Effects of Coping Response on Stress'. In his experiments Dr Weiss subjected rats to electric shocks in unpredictable intervals under two conditions. In the first condition the rats could turn off the low voltage electricity that tickled their little feet by pushing a button inside their cage. In the other condition the rats were wired (yoked) to the first group, and would receive the same amount of electricity (the stressor) as that group, because the button in their cages was only a 'mock' button and pushing it had no effect on the electrical flow under their feet. While both groups effectively received the same amount of electric stimulation at unpredictable times, only the first group had control over its duration, once they worked out the purpose of the button. The yoked rats by contrast could only suffer in silence, the length of time they suffered depended on the rats they were yoked to and how quickly they turned off the electric flow.

In a third group the rats were simply kept in a cage without being subjected to electrical stimulation. This control group provided a baseline of the impact of being kept in a cage.

Following the experiment the rats in both groups were sacrificed (a quaint psychological term for killed) and lesions in their stomachs were measured. The rats in the first group had about three times the number of lesions compared to the control group. However, the yoked rats, with neither predictability nor control over their fate, had almost three times the lesions of the rats in the first group.

Having determined the measurable result of stress as the number of stomach lesions due to the stressor (the electric current), this finding made for a very simple formula:

Unpredictability + (real or perceived) Lack or Loss of Control = Stress

In simple terms this means the more we can predict our fate, and the higher the level of control we can exercise over what happens to us, the less we feel the effects of physiological stress.

This formula is of utmost importance and underlies almost every aspect of this book.

As far as the relationship to fear is concerned we can now say lack of control (real or perceived) and unpredictable conditions trigger fear, which in turn results in the release of hormones and a state we experience as stress.

To be clear, I'm talking about stress of the unpleasant variety — the one we try to escape and reduce through often very maladaptive means such as alcohol or other drugs. Even though ultimately not effective, we often keep using them because they seem more tolerable than the stress we're trying to alleviate. We'll discuss 'positive' stress a little later.

Stress = energy

We've seen that stress is a reaction to unpredictable and uncontrollable situations. In his experiment Dr Weiss demonstrated that lesions occurred in the rats' stomachs when they were exposed to what we now call stress. But how do we know this isn't simply a psychological construct, as for example, the concept of personality? While we can describe personality and ascribe it particular traits, we can't physically place it anywhere in the body. It only exists as a name we give to what we observe. Is it the same for what we call stress, or is there a way of measuring it objectively?

We touched earlier on how a baby develops in the womb and during its infant years. In a way early childhood development, starting in *utero*, seems to replicate human development through the millennia. On our march from one-celled organism to sophisticated *homo sapiens* who managed to fly to the moon and back (apologies to any conspiracy theorists who believe the moon landing was faked), we underwent remarkable changes, which are reflected in the way our brain developed and now operates.

The development of the structures in the limbic system represented a remarkable upgrade of the fight or flight response, and significantly improved the chance of survival. We could now compare incoming sensory input against our database of prior experiences, determine if a threat was involved, and prepare for defence or to run away.

In essence, that was all that was needed for the brain to do its job effectively. What was added after that, such as the neocortex, simply helped spruce up the system, make it faster, more effective and efficient, thereby raising the stakes from survival to improving the chance for dominance, which further improved the chance of not only the survival of the individual, but also the species.

As a lover of cars I can see a distinct parallel with the invention and development of the car. A modern-day vehicle is more comfortable than an old A Model Ford; it's more efficient, faster and has greater technology. Yet both still run on the same principle — burning fuel to turn a crankshaft that converts the vertical energy of pistons going up and down into rotary energy making the wheels go round and propelling the car forward. Except in the modern car more things can go wrong. What an apt analogy to the human brain!

Frustratingly, though, any car big or small, expensive or cheap, can only take you from one place to another and only as fast as the traffic or the speed limit allows. Travelling at 100 km/h is just as fast in a luxury car as it is in an old bomb.

As for development of the human brain, after having the limbic (warning) system in place, every further addition, while being a valuable add-on to the overall survival mechanism, doesn't add much to our choices when under threat of being attacked. When confronted by a physical threat all the sophistication provided by the neocortex, such as your ability to recite the works of Shakespeare or calculate the boundaries of the universe, will come to nothing against the might of a grizzly bear or the speed of a bullet. Your survival comes down to two familiar options: fight or flight. And either of these options results in the same requirement — energy.

I'm highlighting this most basic of realities because it's so easily forgotten. Whatever we do, think and feel, as far as our system is concerned, are all 'actions', and therefore dependent on the availability and supply of energy. If availability or supply is interrupted, it's a simple and practical matter of 'hope it doesn't hurt too much'.

This effectively means energy enables survival and is only released to the degree it's necessary, so there's enough when needed to run or fight. When our survival is being threatened additional energy is made available through the activation of the limbic system, which initiates the release of stress hormones.

Threat → stress = energy → emotions (expressed and released in an action)

Stress is the process that drives our actions and underlies what we then experience as emotions.

The significance of this sequence will become apparent in the next chapter. However, because stress plays such a pivotal role not only in relation to emotions, but also with regard to boundaries, there are a number of other aspects we still have to consider.

Before doing so, there is a third option to the fight or flight response: the 'freeze' response. Young offspring, and defenceless animals adopt this tactic, especially when the predator is one not interested in lifeless prey or carrion. While they may take the 'frozen' animal in their fangs and pummel it a bit they are likely to drop it again when it doesn't move and walk away in search of more lively prey.

We can also observe the freeze response in humans and it's often evident in such statements as *I was so stunned I just couldn't move or say anything* or people who witness an unfolding tragedy without any attempt to help, and simply stand there watching, as if frozen.

Although freezing is an option, it's really more of a last resort, since you put your life in someone else's fangs, so to speak. But if neither running nor fighting is a realistic option and would only amount to the same result (certain death), you may prefer one last roll of the dice.

The 'trickle' effect

Since Dr Weiss's rat experiments, we've discovered our system also undergoes a number of other changes due to stress.

We now know that when subjected to stressors, blood pressure and heart rate increase, skin conductance increases due to sweat being excreted and, according to new research findings, even the state of your arteries and the level of cholesterol they contain change, and have been identified as indicators of stress.

One way of illustrating stress is the example of a battery. If it's trickle-fed by a solar cell it can power a simple fairy light for a very long time. If a second fairy light, and subsequently more little fairy lights are added, the ratio of what I take out and what the solar cell feeds back in becomes an important factor in how long the battery will be able to supply the lights with electricity. If I now add another chain of small, low-watt lights, the battery life will be shortened. Now it's only a matter of time before the battery runs out and nothing works anymore. At some point one more teeny, weeny little light will cause the whole chain of fairy lights to go dark.

We can compare the body to a battery, since it's our power supply and works in a similar fashion to a battery. If too many, or very potent, stressors are applied, be it physically or psychologically, we break down mentally or physically — or both. Our ability to tolerate stressors depends on the level of mental and physical resources at our disposal.

Because we're only human and our resources are limited, each and every one of us has a breaking point. A greater ability to absorb stressors simply means the breaking point for that individual is moved, not removed.

If we take more out of our system than we put back in we get ever closer to the point where nothing works anymore. You can't become motivated. No interest in much at all, tired, just hanging in there by the skin of your teeth. Sound familiar? At this stage your response to the demands made on your resources would probably be diagnosed as depression.

While any demand on the system is a stressor, we may not necessarily experience it as a state of stress. As long as it's within the scope of what we can do we might call it 'a challenge' and may even be eager to take it on. But when the demand approaches the limit of what we have at our disposal we experience it as increasingly adverse, since it is perceived as a threat to the system, which means we're not safe anymore and our survival is at risk.

We now also have the answer to our earlier question — whether or not stress is a psychological construct. It's in fact the measurable response our system produces to try to ensure our survival.

This use of resources applies to any activity where an action takes place inside the body and energy is drained from the battery. For example, the process of thinking means neurons fire — and this firing has to be enabled by an energy source. The more deeply or intensely we think, the more energy the brain requires to meet that task. This energy comes from the same source our muscles take it from: food, which is converted into glucose and then becomes useable energy.

To be physically exhausted from a lot of brainwork is therefore hardly surprising, yet many people seem to ignore or even deny cognitive activity as being a physical activity. While we've abandoned Cartesian dualism, whereby the body and mind are considered separate and based on different mechanisms, the idea still lives on in our daily lives and we often continue to treat them as separate entities.

The cumulative effect resulting in stress is in line with the mechanical, physical perspective the term originates from. A bridge, for example, is constructed to sustain a particular maximum downward pressure. Once that boundary or limit is approached or exceeded, the outcome is unpredictable. It may absorb the extra weight for a short while or it may collapse immediately, due to wear and tear that has weakened its structure over time.

There's an important difference, though, between a structure's ability and the human ability to withstand stressors. While a physical structure is calculated to operate within predetermined limits and fixed parameters, the stress we experience as humans can't be universally defined. It not only depends on the nature of a particular stressor, but also its timing (too many little stressors within a short period of time can also do the trick), and the circumstances when we're confronted with a particular stressor, before we have a stress reaction. We can therefore suddenly feel stressed by events we previously dealt with without raising a sweat and everyone, including ourselves, seems surprised at our 'stress reaction'.

Dr Weiss essentially reduced the occurrence of stress to two factors: unpredictability and loss or lack of control. While this may seem a little reductionist, it's not all that surprising since, from a survival point of view, both have a high 'threat value'.

Think of our ancestors walking through the jungle searching

for food, at the same time having to be alert not to become a tasty morsel for another predator themselves. An attack is possible at any moment, but they have no idea when and where it might come from. How would you feel? A bit anxious?

This constant unpredictability — will I find food or be food? — results in what we would call today stress, but is just another name for energy requirement, either to find or to avoid becoming food. It's all about survival: *Tell me where the attack is coming from, so I can be prepared, one way or the other.*

Although we may not often be in mortal danger these days, we still encounter situations that can be stressful. Travellers who have visited certain countries will know how stressful it can be having to be constantly mindful of your watch, wallet and other items in order to not have them pickpocketed. This sense of needing to protect your belongings can significantly interfere with your wish to capture a special moment on camera or thoughts of what you're going to have for dinner.

What about control? Not having control means being at the mercy of others. If we subject ourselves to such a situation voluntarily, we accept this is the case. In fact, we're in control in a way, because we made the decision to submit to someone else, or fate, and accept the consequences. Flying in a plane is an example for both situations, surrendering control to the pilot and accepting the consequences. Spare a thought for the poor individuals who suffer from a fear of flying. They're expected to surrender their control to someone they don't know, to a contraption they don't trust to stay above the clouds, and are supposed to ignore their concerns.

The feeling of not being in control presents a threat to our survival, because we can't foresee how it's all going to pan out. As the feeling of having no control over a situation becomes stronger, so do our attempts to regain control and we grow more desperate with each attempt. The more this proves a fruitless exercise the more frustrated we become, which leads to more (fruitless) efforts and an ever deeper feeling of despair. Even worse, our attempts may create and leave even bigger problems in their wake, which then frustrate us even more. The vicious circle starts to close in on itself. How many situations spring to mind that you could put in that category?

The (not so) trivial difference

It's often difficult (if not altogether impossible) to determine an objective measure of what is and is not, or *should not*, be stressful. This is closely linked to the *why* when we're feeling stressed in the absence of any discernible good-enough reason. In a way we're now looking at the complimentary element of the 'trickle effect'. What seems like a trivial difference is rightfully called the *just noticeable difference* — and here's my first encounter with it.

As a student of psychology it was a requirement to subject myself to a number of experiments. In my very first exposure we measured the distance an object had been moved, before the person noticed, known as the 'jnd', short for just noticeable difference. What I saw then as something contrived to keep psychology students busy, I've since come to appreciate as one of the fundamental concepts underlying human interactions. It's not the big changes that affect our lives; it's the small ones that can have big effects over time. Which means that if you change your point of view just a little because of reading this book, it can have remarkable effects on the quality of your daily life.

As far as stress is concerned, let me use the diagram on the following page to demonstrate the jnd:

There is often little noticeable difference between the individual stressors (1, 2 and 3); however, somewhere along the ascent to number 10 you'll realize how far you've come on the way to feeling stressed compared to how you felt at point 1, 2 or 3 and your baseline. Of course, depending on the nature of the stressor it could well send you straight up to 10, but in that case you would hardly be surprised (think of *You're fired!* or *I want a divorce* sent via text message), and would be well aware of the reason you feel immediately stressed 'right out of your head'.

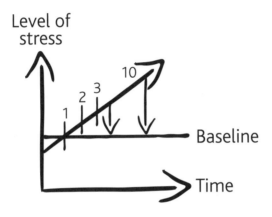

The effects of stress on cognition

If you feel this is a simplification of the wonderful functioning of the human body I would have to agree. Yet instead of making life easier, millions of years of evolution have resulted in a complexity that at times seems to be counterproductive. Rather than having more clarity and — through the variety of options available to us — making more informed choices, we often have difficulties understanding our own actions and why we acted the way we did. Conversely, we can sometimes be surprised to find we acted totally differently from the way we intended to, again wondering how we ended up doing exactly the opposite of our intentions.

The more intimidating a situation becomes, the more our focus shifts. Think of the way our pupils dilate to increase our visual perception; now picture your whole mind as a multifocal camera lens. Imagine being out in the wilderness and scanning the horizon for your love interest to appear. You suddenly hear an unfamiliar sound and you're unsure if it presents a potential threat.

From the wide-angle setting for scanning the countryside your lens now goes into zoom mode, focusing entirely on the sound the potential threat poses. You zoom in on where the danger is coming from. The more interesting or threatening the object appears, the more you zoom in and whatever you have in your sight becomes not only clearer but also bigger and more detailed. By now, however, what you have gained in detail, you have lost in perspective and vice versa. There's nothing good or bad about this, since both settings have their benefits and disadvantages.

Ultimately this magnification is also the mechanism that causes what we know as anxiety and depression. While these labels often refer to a particular disposition or mood state, I here refer to the behaviour we can observe and may consider 'out of proportion', not the subjective emotional state only the individual experiences.

As long as your lens is on zoom the threat is real, regardless of the perspective of a bystander, who might judge the situation as perhaps not desirable but nonetheless easily manageable. Unless you're able to change your lens setting, your misguided system tells you what to do, which means you protect yourself the best way you can and resist all attempts by others who urge you to change your mind. If anything, you might consider these attempts a further threat.

Now add the human perspective

While the fight or flight mechanism may explain what occurs in the brain when we want to run or fight, figuring out what exactly triggered this response and why we reacted to something all of a sudden when we tolerated the same situation previously, can still cause great consternation.

It seems the ongoing sophistication of the brain over the millennia has a lot to answer for — but has evolution erred? I'd say not at all. Just as the addition of a new program increases a computer's usefulness, it also means the program can now clash with other installations, more areas for malfunctions are opened up, new viruses can affect the whole system and so on. The brain isn't much different. With each layer of complexity evolution added, it also made our decisions ever more unpredictable.

The limbic system acts as the alarm centre by warning and preparing us for action. These days, of course, we've many more choices at our disposal than running away or fighting.

However, the actions we choose in response to anything we don't like — let's call it that for simplicity's sake — still fall within the domain of either fight or flight. Pleading with someone, for example, can be a way to assuage an aggressor or a delaying tactic, the *circling and sniffing* of the opponent. If my pleading is unsuccessful I'll still do one or the other: withdraw from the situation or in desperation opt for a hopeless fight.

Some responses are the result of a cognitive component in the (very quick) assessment of a situation following an initial impulse to act in an aggressive or protective manner — the 'on second thought' reactions. They're no longer the immediate reaction of our ancestors to a perceived threat, but instead are mediated by a cognitive process that leads us to perhaps fight verbally (argue) rather than enter into a physical confrontation.

Despite this option we often find ourselves questioning the state of someone's mind, even if it's only our own. If we could only stop and think that what we're feeling is *simply energy*, as has been discussed earlier. That instead of these outbursts we can make a decision and *choose* our course of action rather than feeling helpless and at the mercy of this energy. So why don't we?

The neocortex provides us with an ability to critically think and evaluate our own actions and those of others. If thinking happens before the event, we call it planning. It's when we (re-)act without planning that we find we're often clueless about what just happened. The reason for this is that when we look back we apply the same rational reasoning as when we (rationally) plan our actions. After the event we can't marry the outcome with our previously proven ability to act more wisely.

If we try to explain, often the best we can come up with is 'my emotions got the better of me', which sounds more like a weak attempt to find an excuse rather than an explanation. However, perhaps without knowing it, you're on the right track. And here's the reason why.

When something unexpected or unpleasant happens around us and the (limbic) threat centre responds by initiating the release of stress hormones, thousands of years of brain development are wound back, our survival mechanism takes over and our rational brain takes leave. Put a gun to the head of a very intelligent individual and you'd see the same panicky reaction in their eyes as in the rest of us less intelligently endowed. Apart from the physiological symptoms of sweat pouring out, increased heart activity, dilated pupils and so on, the zoom mechanism would set in.

Instead of thinking of something to do or say that might save them, the person could panic and is likely to do stupid things, such as trying to wrest the gun out of the attacker's hand. That could result in being shot, even if the gun was only meant as a threat.

Often to our detriment, we use that 'zoom' mode on a daily basis without even noticing. Every time we feel threatened in any way, we focus our attention on that object or person and our lens changes from wide-angle to zoom. This could take the form of picking on the particular words someone uses, taking sentences apart to prove that what we perceived is correct ('I'm right and you're wrong'), or 'zooming in' on someone's facial expression, posture or whatever arouses our suspicion.

The worrying aspect is that we don't notice we're now operating on a very primitive level of our mental abilities, simply to protect ourselves from a threat that may not even exist. If we could only stop and think!

To do that we would have to engage a different area of the brain. Instead of staying in the emotional, quite primitive part, we would have to move the activity 'up there' into the neocortex, the upper layer and specifically the left, rational side of the brain.

However, arousal (that is, limbic activity) interferes with this process, and as we now have seen for a good reason, because when the 'alarm centre' in the brain is activated nothing much else matters and brain activity is 'down regulated' which means instead of cortical activity 'up there', the signal goes to the adrenal glands 'down there', where they are located near the kidneys, and the 'flight or fight' response is activated. (That they are 'down there' is due to the fact we used to be much smaller and this area much closer to our head. As we increased in size, the distance between head and adrenal glands also increased.)

From this point on our animal roots show themselves and we act because of the perceived threat — for our own reasons and based on the lessons life has taught us. This could be the lesson we previously learnt with a particular person, or something totally unrelated but reminiscent of an unpleasant memory. When such an experience is reactivated, our limbic system fires up and we send out the message 'Stay away from me, or else . . .' This may be expressed in subtle, civil ways, but can then quickly take the form of more explicit behaviour such as threats or physical aggression.

As the threat continues, and more adrenaline and cortisol flush through the system, the more it affects our ability to think. It also affects our memory. The latter more due to the stress hormone cortisol, which seems to interfere with hippocampal activity, and the ability to store events in short-term memory.

The more 'energized' (stressed) we are, the less likely we are to act rationally, or correctly recall details of an incident. It's one of the frightening aspects in eye-witness testimonies: how 'stressed' the observer was when they saw the incident will determine the reliability of their testimony. Just as surprising is that the witness — in their own mind — will swear to what they 'saw', totally convinced of their (objectively) false memory. Controlled experiments have shown people are still incredulous, even when confronted with video evidence to the contrary.

We can conclude a direct relationship between stress level and left brain activity. As the stress level goes up our cognitive abilities suffer and go down. Conversely, the less stressed we are, the more rationally we can act.

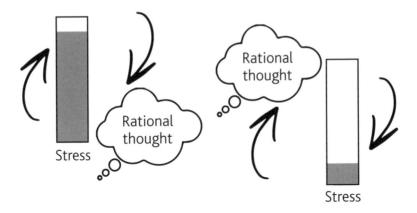

We'll encounter this diagram again when we talk about emotions, and how they affect our ability to think clearly.

Good or bad stress?

Before we get to that question let's make one thing clear: stress is an adaptive response and part of the body's natural alarm system. Adrenaline is always present in us; it's the release of *additional* adrenaline and cortisol we're talking about here and which serves two purposes: to activate the survival mechanism, then release the energy it helps produce to get rid of the stressor. It's the extent and duration that determine the damaging effect stress can exert on us.

Surely there's a difference between good and bad stress, between dealing with some kind of disaster and planning a wedding? Most certainly! But then again, how many weddings do you think you could enjoy planning before it becomes a 'stressful' experience?

Can there be too much good stress? As far as our physiology is concerned, it hardly matters *why* we get excited. When the body perceives a demand on its energy resources, it has to produce the energy to meet that demand. The fact we may enjoy the activity is secondary, and hence people die from heart attacks even though they may have been positively stressed — 'doing what they loved' as it's referred to in the subsequent eulogy. So there can certainly be too much of a good thing when it comes to stress.

The difference between good or bad (damaging) stress is probably best described as the degree to which we experience stressful events. The closer the demand on our resources comes to our finite ability to meet it, the more we're likely to experience this as negative stress.

In other words, we tend to call good stress anything we can handle or enjoy doing, and bad what we don't like or experience as beyond our capacity. However, this is our psychological appraisal; the physiological state of the body is the same in both cases.

Even good stress can be too physically demanding and thereby detrimental to our health. Except we enjoy it and don't call it stress.

Stress in perspective

Stress is often blamed for causing all kinds of illnesses, even cancer. This is a misconception. It's not the stress, but the effects stress has on your system that's causing problems. By weakening your body's defences, the effects of stress may mean you then don't have the resources to fight off an infection or your system succumbs to an attack by cancer cells.

On a practical level this might not sound like much of a difference. Where it can make a difference, however, is in prevention. Recognizing your high level of stress will allow you to bring it down before your immune system has to fend off any attacks.

We're faced with the reality that the symptom is not the enemy. It's an ally. Fighting the symptom is akin to shooting the messenger.

Part 2 will outline some strategies for how to avoid and deal with stressors.

4. **Emotions**

When we hear someone say 'Gee, did he get angry!' it doesn't really tell us what the person did when he was angry, and also pre-empts our own judgment about what kind of emotion was at work. We're already told he was angry. In reality he may have panicked, because he imagined an attack that didn't occur, but to the observer he was 'angry'.

This confuses an action and the emotion we infer from it; the energy we think is driving the action becomes the action itself. If a person is seen to be angry, she would have demonstrated that in some observable way, how else would we otherwise know she was angry?

However, we've seen how the limbic system reacts to protect you by initiating the release of stress hormones to prepare the system for defence against a real or perceived threat. When stress hormones are present in the system the body assumes danger is imminent.

For some, even hearing the word 'no' can be perceived as a threat; it means a plan is being crossed, an anticipated goal is at risk and satisfaction or having fun is jeopardized. That goes for children as much as for adults.

Any complex situation usually comes about through a combination of simple, single intersecting facts or issues. When two people come together the seed for complexity is sown, be it through different interests, goals, values, priorities, or simply the right thing happening but at the wrong time. Despite this range of differences, however, almost every aspect can be explained by their individual and necessarily different backgrounds.

The simplicty in complexity

Why is it easy to become lost in a maze? Because all the tunnels are crooked and there are many obstacles in the way? Mazes in which I have lost my way were no obstacle course; in fact, they were only at worst slightly curved walkways. The complexity came not from the difficulty of the maze's components — tunnels, dead-ends and walkways — but from how they were or were *not* connected.

The brain itself can be easily understood when each individual neuron, its function and nature, is observed. What is less understood is how these neurons function together — their interconnectedness — and the way the brain builds, organizes, extends, manages and activates them, which is further complicated by the fact that the same connections can be involved in very different contexts and meet apparently quite unrelated demands.

The way neurons form connections and fire under certain circumstances but not others makes for a (very) complex system. In other words, complexity arises from simplicity.

Without finding the boundary where each neural activity starts, changes or connects and another commences, it would be impossible to establish how networks form and operate.

Emotions — the unreasonable force

When Descartes declared *cogito ergo sum* — I think, therefore I am — he set the trend for Western philosophy and the supreme role 'reason' is now afforded in science and research. A mathematician as well as philosopher, Descartes discarded perception as unreliable, developed the distinction between mind and body known as Cartesian dualism, and proposed that the mind generally controls the body. However, the body can also exercise influence over the otherwise rational mind, such as when people act out of passion or irrationally.

It was not until science and the development of new technologies such as Magnetic Resonance Imaging (MRI) and Positron Emission Tomography (PET) scans enabled a better understanding of the brain's functioning that we came to accept there is no such dualism. Rather than the body being the physical entity and the mind an almost mysterious phenomenon, the latter is simply the functioning of the brain, which in turn is part of the physical body. Just as walking is a function of the legs.

While this is now the scientifically accepted position, the underlying idea is harder to kill and when we talk about the mind, it's often still with a reverence otherwise mostly reserved for the unknown and poorly understood. When we talk about emotions it gets even fuzzier. What are they? Where do they come from?

While we all experience feelings (I use feelings and emotions interchangeably) we can't define them in the same way we describe a physical object. We may be able to refer to a sensation we share with other human beings, but describing it is a different story. How would you describe your pain? Emotions can't be observed, measured or tasted and yet, we can't deny their reality, at least on the level an individual experiences them. It's impossible to qualify or quantify an emotion so that you can experience it in its exact nature and quality as I do.

Although we may use the same words to describe them, what we mean isn't always that clear-cut. More importantly, it's often neither maliciously nor with ill intent that we misunderstand or are misunderstood — it's often our own inability or unwillingness to accept the other person's perception as having the same value as our own.

Why do we find it so difficult to define emotions? That it's impossible can be deducted from the millions of songs about love. They all emphasize a different experience of the same emotion, and if it were easy to define surely we would only need one song about love that would say it all.

While people all over the world tend to have very similar facial expressions for a particular emotion, the depth of those emotions is indescribable. And I can never — never ever — feel exactly what you feel.

The same emotion experienced by different people is the same in name only and can at best be shared in nature, not in degree.

There's a simple explanation for this. Imagine comparing a child who grows up in the middle of the African jungle with one raised in an urban jungle. Would they have the same experiences, and react to the same situations in exactly the same way? The answer seems obvious. Their responses to a particular challenge will depend on the experiences they confronted when they were growing up. Their individual environment would foster a particular perception most suitable for survival and expand or restrict their choices accordingly. In addition, the influence of their parents and the social expectations of their peers would make certain choices more palatable than others. The sum of these influences arising either as a result of 'nature' or 'nurture' practices might even determine whether they perceive a particular circumstance as a challenge at all. This, then, is the psychological explanation for *why* we experience emotions differently.

As such it's also subject to different opinions about which influence is to blame for the fact that one person remains totally unaffected by an event while everyone around them is in danger of drowning in a sea of their own tears. (What a soggy way to go!)

All of which poses another interesting question.

Why are some people more easily spooked than others?

Why do people react differently in the face of similar stressors and why can that reaction by itself be a stressor for people around them? The answer has two parts. One relates to the *why*, the other to the *when*.

The *why*

The amygdala assesses incoming information to the brain and determines what is and is not a threat. But how does it know one from the other? While the brain as a physical structure is fully formed at birth, its functions develop at different rates. In line with the evolutionary development of the brain, the reptilian and most primitive part of the brain is always present and functioning, maintaining breathing and other essential functions. By contrast, the limbic system and neocortex are present but need input to function, much like a new computer needs various programs in order to operate.

For the limbic system, in particular the amygdala, this input is provided by the experiences to which a baby is exposed and the feelings those experiences evoke. This occurs over the first three years in life, at which point the rational brain starts to come on-line. The human brain has grown in size over the past few hundred thousand years, until it became too big for a woman's pelvis. It's for this reason we're all born prematurely, compared to other animals, and before our brain is fully developed.

So while present as a structure, the neocortex becomes active at about the age of three years when the ability to use information, the ability to 'think' finally kicks in and develops at an accelerating rate. It has been suggested that in the first six years, the brain creates more neural connections than during the rest of our lives.

From the moment we're born we start to take in information. Because our rational brain isn't working yet, we perceive the events around us according to their emotional value. These events with emotional significance are stored and provide the limbic system with the information it then compares with new incoming stimuli. The significance, this emotional tag, also tells the system to fire when triggered accordingly, putting in place the necessary mechanisms we know as 'stress reactions', if the experience warrants this.

Because this process starts at the earliest stage of development the importance and significance analysts such as Freud and, more recently, neuropsychologists have attached to it is understandable. As the footings of any construction determine the structural safety of the completed building when exposed to storms and other external impacts, early childhood experiences influence the way the adult is able to accept and deal with challenges. While a faulty footing doesn't cause a house to fall over at any moment, it carries that risk if a storm or flood hits. In other words, it's more vulnerable.

If a child's early environment is pleasant, free of overwhelming stressors and relatively predictable, that child will experience the world as a safe place. A peaceful and predictable environment is likely to produce a less reactive, more 'relaxed' amygdala, one that allows neurons to sprout and the brain to develop to its potential.

If, however, the child's world is upset by many changes or they are exposed to their parents' screaming and fighting (or think of a child growing up in war-torn surroundings), the young brain is flooded with stress hormones. The result could be a highly strung, very shy and withdrawn individual or someone we may perceive as aggressive, judged by the way they release their high level of adrenaline.

A wildly over-active amygdala is concerned in the first instance with securing survival and is therefore always on the lookout for danger signs and preparing for the worst. This constant state of activation inhibits neural growth and the development of a healthy network of neural pathways.

Other factors of course, also play a significant role, such as a genetic predisposition or the parents' propensity to be highly reactive and worried or, conversely, laid-back and adaptive. The child learns from all these experiences and each contributes to shape their view of the world and their immediate environment, how to react, what to do and what to avoid. According to this early learning, called *implicit memory*, the amygdala is set to react to the events the child has experienced as undesirable or potentially dangerous.

Without these emotional tags our experiences are simply facts, much like mathematical equations or grammatical rules. As you may have noticed, these are all the activities we associate with the left brain, no emotions attached.

Like a computer, the amygdala is now supplied with emotional information about the outside world, but still reacts to any potential threat in accordance with the way it's been programmed. Another way of looking at it is to think that the experiences a baby is exposed to provide them with the glasses through which they see the world. The baby will subsequently see the world as dangerous, trustworthy, predictable, chaotic — or all of the above — at different times, depending on what their early experiences have taught. So, this answers *why* the amygdala fires; now for the question of *when*.

The *when*

Let's compare the amygdala to a light switch. As we've seen, when triggered it responds in predetermined ways. The baby's experiences now add the setting of the 'sensitivity sensor' (like the kind that lights up when you walk past it).

Depending on the input the child has received, the intensity of the experience and the emotional threat value attached to it, this trigger can be set at a very low threshold and the proverbial feather sets it off or, conversely, triggers can be set at very high thresholds and much wild flailing of arms is needed before the light eventually comes on. Once the trigger is activated the system then releases the stress (activation) hormones.

The role of the primary caregiver is vitally important to this process of setting the child's sensitivity level. Control of emotions, or the energy they represent, occurs first through the primary caregiver — usually the mother. When they model behaviour the baby responds, to which the mother responds. This co-regulation between mother and child results in those 'implicit memories' and our unreflected, involuntary responses, attitudes and reactions to events and challenges.

Likewise, our wants and needs — too often also associated with strong emotions — are shaped by the experiences early life provides and determine what we want to achieve, avoid or possess at any cost, throughout childhood and adult life. While the reason and foundation for these needs and wants is laid down early, it receives more detailed shape later through the way we try to achieve what we want — and are successful or unsuccessful in doing so. It's also shaped by how the world around us reacts to our endeavours. This teaches us to be more cunning, careful, ruthless, accommodating or discerning when pursuing what we think is the road to our happiness. In other words, the world around us initially shapes the way we pursue what we hope brings us happiness. Eventually we may change the goals we set for ourselves, but there's no guarantee we actually do this, because that involves a conscious effort and a rational decision. Some folks pursue the same elusive dream forever, driven by the unconscious desire to heal the hurt and pain someone inflicted on them a long, long time ago.

While the left brain develops at a truly breathtaking rate, the 'emotional brain' almost stagnates. How we feel, what we feel and how we react emotionally to different stimuli is laid down at that very early stage of brain development. As far as emotional learning is concerned, once you experience emotions there's not much more to learn. There is no way to experience them 'better' or more efficiently. This is quite different for the left, rational brain, which can learn to react differently to different emotions, change the behavioural pattern, or decide not to react at all.

There is no limit to the amount of information the left brain can acquire, while emotions will always be present in one way or another at the basic level we experienced them already as a baby. Even when dementia has set in and the functions of the rational brain are all but unrecognisable, there are still expressions of fear, pleasure or dislike.

Misplaced blame

The early childhood experiences that form the brain are also responsible for the fact that we later believe others can make us happy and responsible for the way we feel.

Picture the following: baby plays happily and decides that the most interesting thing to do would be to poke their little fingers into a power point. But what does the mother do? She yells loudly, and yanks the baby's hand away from the excitement, in the process spoiling all the fun to be had.

Apart from the baby's reaction to such treatment (who needs

spoilsports with friends like that!), the baby will also notice the resulting feeling from such interference. While having just felt quite excited, the baby now feels sad, disappointed, generally not good. And it was Mum who caused this feeling, hence the infantile, albeit understandable conclusion: 'Mum made me feel bad'.

While understandable from a baby's perspective, we unfortunately keep hanging on to this belief even as adults. So, I guess it's time to grow up, hard as it may be to say goodbye to this long-held and cherished belief that served us so well when we wanted to blame someone for our feelings.

More Beast than Beauty — meet your emotional brain

A way to understand the often used distinction between right and left brain activity is to think of the right brain as the 'original' brain, to which the limbic system projects its activity and which we now associate with 'emotions'. The left by contrast, is pre-occupied with its different functions, namely rational thought, rather than (instinctual) reactions.

When a light-switch is flicked it lets electric current flow, which then turns on the light, no matter if it's dark or daylight. Likewise, when activated the amygdala fires and doesn't distinguish between a real or perceived threat (think of practical jokes), nor does it discern the nature of the threat.

Applied to interpersonal situations, when I hear my partner disagree with me it could stand for a number of different 'threats'; for example, she wants to leave me, or would not defend me if I were attacked. Jealousy, apart from the more sophisticated psychological explanations, can simply be a reaction to a threat to my gene pool. If someone else messes around with my partner, it affects the survival of my own genes, at least from a male perspective. For the female it could mean that feeding as well as protecting her young is going to be more difficult without the help of a partner. On the very first level of analysis it's an instinctive reaction, and happens before any religious or social aspects enter the equation.

Fear causes limbic system activity and the body builds up energy to be able to take whatever action is required. We saw this in the equation:

Threat → stress = energy → emotions → action

The question now is how is this arousal, this energy released? We often equate 'arousal' with sexual activity, which is generally associated with a pleasurable state. This association may therefore blind us to the fact that arousal can actually be quite unpleasant. Even, or especially, during sexual arousal, we seek release. It's the whole point of the exercise, physiologically speaking. In fact, it's the role of 'arousal' to initiate relief from this very state. Strange as it may sound, it announces 'Now that I'm here, get rid of me'. Compare it to a fire alarm bell. When it rings it alerts you to attend to a fire, so you can turn off the annoying and noisy alarm.

Arousal is the alarm bell that alerts our system to prepare for some physical 'task'.

Another form of arousal, 'stage fright', demonstrates our delicate relationship with adrenaline and arousal. An insufficient degree of arousal results in an unanimated, even boring performance; too much, and you're likely to forget your lines or miss your cue to get on stage altogether because you're being sick backstage.

Previously, our only two options were running or fighting when adrenaline strikes. This is the body's physiological response. As we've seen, this repertoire has been significantly enriched. When we become frustrated we can slam a door or scream out loud. You may even recall incidents when you were so frustrated you started to cry. Think of young children who can't do anything else but cry to express their frustration, while later they may throw things on the floor when 'angry' (aroused) or in frustration of being misunderstood, not getting what they want or feeling unable to express what they feel or need. When we simply observe the behaviour, we don't know what goes on in their young minds. Only when we know the context can we start to guess, because again, we'll never exactly know if it's frustration, anger or sadness that drives their tears. How we deal with our arousal is the psychological aspect of our response, based on what we got away with in the past, what got us what we wanted or whatever else helped us get relief. While we cannot prevent the physiological part, we can control how we deal with it.

When subjected to any emotion, we can run around the block, cry, punch holes in the wall or someone's lights out, or all of the above in no particular sequence. Usually, just one or two of the options will do the trick and help us calm down again. It comes down to individual choices and humans have developed different ways of ridding themselves of the energy their limbic system produces. However, all of these reactions are simply different ways of releasing the energy we've built up following a real or perceived threat.

What constitutes a threat can probably best be understood from the survival function of the brain, which precedes all other processes. Any circumstance, event, action, creature (human or otherwise), associated with unpredictability or over which we have little or no control represents a potential threat causing the release of stress hormones and a state of arousal.

All actions, all human activity, is in the first instance driven by the instinct and aim to survive. Moral and social considerations, altruism, religious beliefs, friendship or fear of consequences may then override this survival instinct and lead us to allow 'women and children first' to enter the life raft. However, not everyone lingers long enough for that thought to interfere with their desire to live and 'every man for themselves' dictates their spontaneous actions.

'Understanding' the emotional brain

What makes the emotional brain so difficult to understand is the built-in difficulty when communicating, or trying to communicate, our emotions. Emotions are a right-brain activity, while our capacity to think, as well as the ability to express these thoughts in words is reserved for the left brain. While the right side is very adept at all things that increase our chance of survival, such as reading non-verbal signals, the left side adds the rational bits. Counting, putting events in sequence, organizing and keeping track of dates, all that is your left brain in action.

Since our emotional brain lacks a concept of time it means that when it experiences a sensation it's all encompassing. It's here and now and as such has a certain quality of *forever*. Of course this isn't in a real sense, since our rational brain may intervene. As an example, think about pain. When we feel pain, our first thought is not *That's okay, it will all be over in a couple of days*. If we think at all it's usually something that happens afterwards and is a coping strategy accompanied by the hope that our estimate about how long the pain will last is correct. What we feel at the time however, is PAIN; whether that be emotional or physical, the thought of its temporal limitation is not part of the immediate experience.

To see the right brain in operation, observe a toddler for a while and then interfere in some way that meets with their disapproval. Even if you only want to join in the game, if you do something that does not fit in with their own ideas, big tears may start rolling down their cheeks within two seconds flat. You then rectify the situation and within another few nanoseconds, the tears are gone again, replaced by joyful giggles and smiles. We may call this 'little prince/ princess syndrome' but it really is only a demonstration of the fact that a young child is a bundle of hypothalamic activity. That is, they are entirely run by their limbic system, which doesn't think or negotiate and has no sense of time. Try telling a toddler Christmas is only two days away! You may as well have called the whole thing off, as far as they're concerned.

Emotions are raw, unmitigated and unlimited in their extent until a little later in life, when the cognitive abilities start to develop. Only when our capacity to think has developed (and to the extent of this development) can we put an event into a particular perspective. At this point we're (theoretically) able to tolerate the situation without being consumed by anxiety, depression or despair.

The operational words of caution above are *to the extent of this development.* As you'll have experienced yourself, at times we can cope quite well with certain stressors, at others we feel overwhelmed by the same demand or crumble under decidedly less pressure. Put differently, at times we have the resources to think about an event before we act, at other times we only react.

Although we talk about the practical application of boundaries in detail in a moment, here is a small example of how setting boundaries could be seen as a way of reminding you to add perspective to your experience. On the neural level it means you add a rational element to the experience, moving the experience from the emotional right brain into the rational left brain. Here you can manipulate the event any way you like. For example, you can remind yourself it doesn't matter, that you'll get your own back in time, that the other person is simply stressed or whatever works best for you when you want to take control over your actions, rather than ride the crest of the waves of your emotions, like flotsam — and simply react without thought.

The association of the right brain with survival indicates that in evolutionary terms it's the older of the two halves. The right brain is also the one that tells us what we want — I refer to it as our *kid's brain*: I want it all and I want it now. I regard it as the closest to Freud's Id in his theoretical model of our psychological make-up. As far as the right brain is concerned it doesn't consider the consequences of its actions, nor the rights and interests of others. In fact, it doesn't think, full stop. To make matters worse, it doesn't have the faculty of speech, the prerogative of the left brain, and can't express or explain why it wants what it does.

It's the left brain (strictly speaking the prefrontal cortex i.e. the new, 'thinking' part of the brain) that's involved in decision-making, putting the brakes on the unrestrained desire to act on the impulse from the right side of the brain; telling you that you can't shoot the person who stepped on your blue suede shoes, as much as you'd like to.

This is the result (or failure as it may turn out) of our social brain, which for the most part holds us back from spontaneous reactions we might later regret when the emotion has given way to more rational thought.

It may be why we consider ourselves rational beings. Since the left brain controls speech and has privileged access to what it wants the world to know, it keeps telling the world — and itself — that humans are rational beings above all. Liar!

Nothing could be further from the truth. Like it or not, we're still the animal of old, much more than we would like to admit. The overriding function of the brain is not to achieve the ability to fly to the moon, but to ensure our survival. When threatened, the right brain takes over and the best the left side can do is try to explain the aftermath.

To put it differently, our right brain has made up its mind about what we're going to do long before the left has had time to make up the explanation (or excuse) for it. This has been shown experimentally. By observing brain activity, researchers could tell long before the subjects made a choice, which option they would exercise. In everyday life we sometimes call it rationalisation, or 'bulldusting' and the process can be painful to watch when someone tries to give a rational explanation for what seems anything but.

The mechanism in the emotional brain works as follows: I really, I mean *really*, want a sports car. Which is OK, except that *want* is the operative word here. Firstly, because this wish is now directing my actions, at this point from the underground or the subconscious. Secondly, because *want* is all I can afford. Then I see this very desirable beauty advertised, and it's cheap — I mean *cheap*. Not buying it would not only be a sin, it would deprive me of the opportunity to make a huge profit when I sell it again in years to come. It's *that cheap*.

While *that cheap* doesn't mean *more affordable*, after throwing the argument around in my head for a while, I come to the logical conclusion I just *have to* buy this car for financial reasons. Not because I always wanted a sports car, I'd even admit this isn't the reason at all anymore, it's simply the only decision that — and here it comes — seems logical and correct.

This is an example of how the right brain achieves what it wants and then dresses it up as a left brain, and therefore a rational, decision.

Expression of emotions

This 'division of labour' into feeling and thinking, with the thinking part having privileged access to speech, has wide-reaching implications. While we're able to feel an emotion, there is no provision to express this feeling directly through words, since the speech centre is on the left-hand side. Small wonder we struggle to say what we feel, I mean *really* feel. Any such attempt can only ever be an approximation of the real emotion. Also remember that words themselves are only representations for the real thing.

Here we are, experiencing a feeling, which we can't directly express but have to transfer to the left side of the brain, which doesn't have the first idea about what an emotion feels like. Instead it has to take the input from the right, is supposed to find a word which expresses this input by searching through its dictionary to find a mental representation resembling what the right brain is conveying and then manage to put it into words so it can be understood.

And after all these efforts, what if you don't speak my language? All my efforts were in vain, that's what! Unfortunately, that's the fate of our emotions — we can't verbally express them the way we experience them. I am fairly sure I'm not the only person who has been in a situation where I might as well have spoken a different language when I tried to express my innermost feelings. This becomes especially obvious — and painfully so — the more emotional investment we have in the person to whom we try to convey what we experience emotionally. Some may associate such experiences with unrequited love, others a lovers' spat, and still others may just call it marriage. For the more successful ones, it means you've now accepted the impossible and settled for making do with the approximation of what you think they meant.

While we may find it difficult, if not impossible to verbally express feelings, we're much better at expressing them in non-verbal language. A touch or a facial expression expresses so much more than words can ever do. If we were able to trust these non-verbal cues we would understand each other emotionally much more accurately.

Alas, we're human and endowed with the faculty of thought, and unfortunately, instead of trusting our feelings we try to make sense of what we perceive with our right brain. We want something more tangible; we see it, hear it, or feel it, only to then dismiss it, because we can't believe our eyes or ears. As Frankie and Nancy (Sinatra) put it: *And then you go and spoil it all by saying something stupid like 'I love you'*. Words get in the way.

What do I make of it? Trusting the often maligned gut feeling and allowing two right brains to communicate with each other is much more direct and honest. Sitting quietly, holding hands and looking deep into each other's eyes had meaning long before it became a movie cliché.

Reason or emotions? A matter of balance

Emotions are the antithesis to reason, and can cause much harm in the way we express them. But as much as that may be the case we wouldn't want to miss them, lest we lose our humanity. They are part of what makes us human. Without them we might as well be robots.

But how do we temper emotions with reason — as much as reason with emotions? How do we get the balance right?

When talking about emotions versus reason it's not helpful to think of them in terms of good or bad. A more productive method is to use the distinctions useful versus unhelpful, because just as you can be too emotional, you can also be too rational.

So, what should you rely on when making decisions?

Decisions commonly have an impact on our lives beyond the moment we make them. It's not good to make decisions when overcome with emotions. Because emotions are fickle, decisions based on emotions are just as fickle. Sometimes when you're told to trust your instincts you can wake up to discover you've fallen for the wrong person — again. As I said, emotions are fickle and don't stack up in the cold light of rational appraisal.

So, let's choose reason then? Not so quick. Go to the extreme of rational thought and you have the manager who fires their staff on Christmas Eve, because *It's as good a time as any and we can start the New Year afresh.* In other words, the typical sociopath, previously known as a psychopath, who has no concept of, or scant regard for, other people and what they consider emotional bubblegum and touchy-feely sentimentalism.

Thanks for nothing, then?

It all comes down to balance when making decisions. If we're totally rational, we can't also be totally emotional — and vice versa. The relationship between emotions and reason is completely negative in statistical terms: as one goes up the other one goes down.

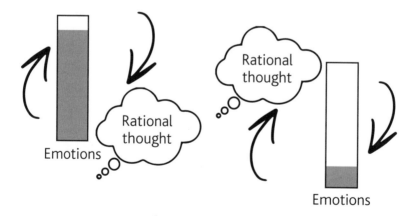

You may also be able to recall an argument you have had with someone close to you. After the heat has gone out of the discussion, reason returns, often accompanied by regret over what was said in the heat of the moment. Many unwanted pregnancies also attest to the fact that as passion rushes in, reason quietly leaves the room, not to return until later — or too late, as the case may be.

The challenge is to have not too much of either. Try to keep the balance by reminding yourself that decisions based on emotions are only good as long as the emotion lasts. Hence the good advice (make that *very* good advice): sleep on it!

Picture emotions as energy and it all starts to make sense. You can then appreciate how your decisions are much more likely to be guided by reason than emotion when the energy has dissipated. As long as emotions (energy) rule they'll influence your decisions towards satisfying your emotional needs, not towards what makes logical sense.

Emotions: asset or liability?

Ask yourself: are my emotions weighing me down or supporting me? I tend to use the following sketch to demonstrate what words may not communicate that well. (By the way, you can replace emotional experiences with life experiences and it works just as well.)

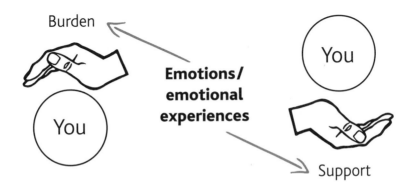

Do I crumble under the weight of my emotions or does the sum of my experiences supply me with the resources to enable me to deal with the challenges I face? It may simply be a matter of flipping from underneath to stand on top. (When I say 'simply' that doesn't imply it's necessarily easy.)

This also applies to what we may consider positive emotions, as they can be just as destructive as negative ones. Of course, emotions are neither positive nor negative. It's how we express them or what we do as a result of experiencing a particular emotion that makes the difference.

Acting under pressure

When I use the word *choice* here it's to emphasise that although we may not consciously decide on a particular action, we nonetheless have other options and *choice* highlights that we're not being damned to a particular action, although it may feel as though we are. If we fall for it, and surrender our control, it can be a fateful deception.

While some readers may accept this without objection, many may reject the notion that decisions made under pressure or coercion are actually their own decisions. Earlier I pointed out the example of heroes who give their lives, because of the choice they make in the face of a threat to their own survival. It does seem to debunk the myth that we've no choice when faced with an act of aggression. There is, however, another way of arriving at the same conclusion other than relying on moral convictions.

A common assumption is that under threat the 'fight or flight' response kicks in and we act without thinking and simply do what comes naturally. We take measure of the enemy and then decide it would be wise to beat a hasty retreat or that this is the time to make a stand (possibly because we're familiar with our shortcomings in the running department) and give it our best shot.

Precisely those programmed options, to run instead of fight or vice versa, indicate we *do* have a choice, like it or not. Even on this most basic level, to run or take a stand logically involves a decision, otherwise we would all react in the same way when facing a threat.

Once the choice is made, though, we then react without further rational thought. If we decide to fight, we do so until the danger has been dispensed with; if we run, it's without consideration of who is next to us (think crowd panic), until we're safe or collapse.

We exercise these nature-given choices every day in many different guises. We may confront a boss or colleague or we may instead decide to go home and kick the dog. You may comfort yourself that *my day will come*, and postpone your action, but you could just as likely tell him what he can do with his (well, really your own) job.

It's tempting to absolve ourselves from the consequences of our actions by asserting that we *didn't have a choice*, because the alternative was too unpalatable to be even considered as a realistic option. This may appease our conscience to some extent but it leaves out the important part — the choice we *did* make even though we may not want to see it as that — and hence we're fooling ourselves. From that moment on we mould the world to suit our own reality, reinterpreting other people's actions to fit the picture we've created in our own minds.

Take an imaginary conversation after a situation where you thought you had no choice and someone questions you about it. It's more likely to become a confrontation than a conversation, because the other person may be pointing out both of your options, while you only see — and defend — the one you took. To make sense of what will appear to you as their *irrational* argument, you'll see it as an attack, or put it down to their stupidity, their animosity, or some other trait within *their* imperfect personality.

This assessment will guide your subsequent interactions with that person, and as you can probably appreciate, it will only be a matter of time before a serious falling-out.

Such situations only make life more complicated than it has to be. We can avoid such complications by simply accepting that every action we take is a choice — even when it looks at the time as though it's the only option we have available.

In that case you may argue that you made the only *reasonable* decision. Being honest with yourself and about the fact you exercised a choice, you can now also be honest with everyone else. You don't have to feel under attack or that you have to defend yourself. You made the best choice available to you and that's that. No need to argue. If anything, you may be interested to learn what others would have done. This willingness to learn can only be generated if your mind is free to do so. In other words, when you don't feel you're under attack. In this state your brain is able to retain and integrate new information.

5. **Emotions, stress and boundaries — the connection**

Before applying a boundary focus to specific situations let me briefly clarify the relationship between emotions and stress, and provide a flowchart that demonstrates the connection between boundaries (or rather their violation) and our stress response.

We've established that emotions evolved from the primeval fight or flight response; if not, we would have to assume that any animal with a limbic system would also experience the range of emotions we proudly call *human* traits.

While this seems to point to a much more sophisticated mechanism in charge of emotions than I have previously suggested, this is fine by me. My position only suggests the limbic system is *involved* in the role emotions play, which allows for future discoveries that may trace in more detail how different emotions are created and experienced. However, this is well beyond the scope of this book.

I also concede that psychological research suggests anxiety, depression and stress are distinct conditions but nonetheless share common features, which I suggest point to a common origin. I propose that the physiological stress response is the first reaction to a stressor, which can lead to a number of different behaviours. It's at that point that a distinction between depression and anxiety occurs. The stress response is really the reaction to an urgent demand for energy, perceived by the brain.

Allow me another analogy. As with any other pastime or activity we engage in, when we have the luxury of time and safety, we refine what we have and what we do with it. The humble car as transport becomes a luxury limousine or sports car we take for rides just for fun. Skiing becomes a status symbol, where the skill is more defined by the outfits than the body movements down the slopes. In short, usefulness is complemented by pleasure maximization. And so it is with the brain, enriched by experiences, it developed more refined mechanisms.

When we combine these concepts — unpredictability, loss of control and the symptoms we describe as feeling stressed — we can now work backwards. Starting with these feelings (depressed, anxious, worried, angry, etc.) they tell us our system is reacting to one or several stressors, which at the most basic level means we perceive a threat to our wellbeing in some way.

We may consider the circumstances that have caused these emotions and, accordingly, attach different names to the behaviour by which these emotions are released. We may also have better honed skills of expressing (or hiding) them, but at the core we'll find the *primitive* areas of the brain in action to meet its primary task of ensuring our survival, because we're either unsure of what will happen (the situation is unpredictable) and/or we feel we have little or no control over the outcome. For example, this may be because the outcome is predictably undesirable, but also unavoidable, or because we can see no alternative or escape from the situation.

On a practical level, when you feel stressed, create some predictability and increase your level of control. It's that easy — in theory. It's not that difficult in practice either, and we'll get to the trick for bringing these changes about in a moment.

The relationship between stress and boundary violation

We've established that when dealing with a situation, striving for a goal or attempting a solution where you have no control over the outcome, you must accept whatever happens and only have to deal with your own feelings about this. You can use coping strategies but you'll not be consumed by your (perceived) failure.

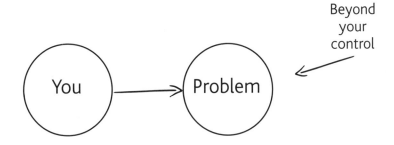

However, if instead you incorporate the problem and make it your own, you've now made something you have no control over part of yourself:

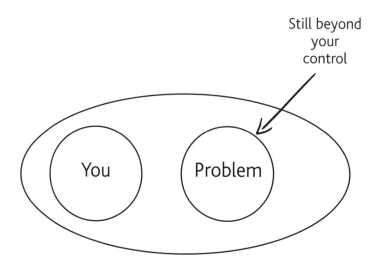

The boundaries have disappeared between the problem and yourself. You're now one with the problem, but you still have no control over it:

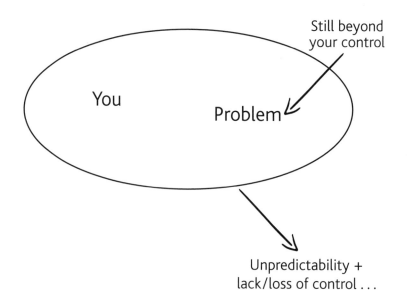

Unpredictability
+ lack/loss of control

↓

Stress = Energy   - anger
released as   - depression   ⎫
what we   - frustration ⎬ aka ——→ **Actions**
know as . . . - sadness   ⎭ **Emotions**

This is a schematic representation of how and why the violation of boundaries leads to stress. Respecting boundaries means accepting that the only control I have is over myself. Conversely, while I can't control other people (which may not stop me from trying), they also can't determine my behaviour or feelings. While I can't hold others responsible for the way I feel, it also means I'm *not* responsible for the way others respond to my actions.

The unavoidable caveat — The Pleasure Principle

As suggested earlier, that fear is the original motivator and ultimately the basis for action is certainly the case for less-developed animal species. The more sophisticated and advanced the organism, the more complex motivators become and the flipside of stress avoidance is the seeking of pleasant states through pleasurable activities, known as 'pleasure maximization'.

In the animal world, we see this when cubs engage in playful behaviours (at least that's the human interpretation), when they roll around on the ground, bite each other cheekily, and crawl over their mother until they receive a painful signal that they're making a nuisance of themselves.

As humans became more dominant and able to survive without having to fend for themselves, they had more time on their hands and could focus increasingly on the pursuit of happiness. However, fear ultimately takes precedence over our need for pleasure. This is what I have in mind when I speak of fear as the motivator for action. When threatened, the pursuit of our survival could probably be regarded as maximizing our pleasure, namely that of staying alive if we survive.

PART 2

Boundaries in action

6. The boundary of a boundary focus

While providing a new way of dealing with issues as they arise, a boundary focus is also useful in resolving messy situations. But before becoming obsessed with boundary setting and observance, keep in mind that something is only a problem if it has become a problem — or, as my mother used to say, *when there is no plaintiff, there is no judge.* When something has become an issue, mentally returning to the basics — *I'm only responsible for my (re-)actions and can't control anything external to myself* — will remind and help you to extract yourself, or reorganize and re-evaluate the relationship, problem or situation from a neutral position. For example, if an invited boundary crossing is no longer welcome, how can you deal with it?

Before continuing I would like to make this point very clear:

To maintain boundaries is helpful, but not a goal. It's a strategy to find a solution if one is needed, not a solution in itself!

My emphasis on the importance of boundaries might be taken as a warning not to become involved with other people — this is *not* the aim.

Relationships are essential to our wellbeing.

As human beings, boundaries define us as individuals and we define ourselves by our relationships. They are there to be respected, not to be avoided. Without crossing boundaries there would be no human interaction, and mankind would become robotic. The mutually agreed crossing of personal boundaries leads to true intimacy. Again, this is not restricted to sexual intimacy, but extends to any friendship or personal relationship.

Am I now taking back what I've been preaching? Not at all. Establishing, or re-establishing boundaries can help us find solutions to problems that have arisen because boundaries have been crossed. Renegotiating the extent or content of boundaries is a significant aspect of relationships that grow in depth and meaning. Redefining boundaries doesn't necessarily mean the inclusions become less and the circles smaller. Boundaries can also be enlarged as familiarity develops and with it a greater tolerance so we can allow each other more freedom within the relationship.

The mutually agreed crossing of our personal boundaries leads to true intimacy, whatever the nature of the relationship. However, when those two circles overlap it carries the potential for discomfort to develop. The idea here is not to avoid such interaction, but to be aware of the pitfalls when making the decision to step into someone's personal zone, even when invited.

This awareness makes it easier to pull back when necessary by simply acknowledging that boundaries have been crossed. Sometimes it may have been an invisible line you've inadvertently overstepped, and the other person has decided to point that out to you. A common reaction is to take such a reaction against boundary crossing as a personal attack. But it's not personal against *you*. It's personal for the person who feels their line has been crossed, and who feels their space has been invaded. It's *their* vulnerability that's been threatened and provoked their reaction, not *yours*.

Rather than judging, simply acknowledge that someone claims back their ground. If you don't like it, pull back as well, and the overlapping circles become separate again. That's *your* option, *your* choice.

Simply a road map

A boundary focus only points into a general direction, not to a particular destination — just like travelling to a foreign country where you've never been before. You may know a particular spot lies in the east or west, but you don't know exactly how to get there. That will be decided when you come closer and you can ask for more specific direction.

In the following chapters I'll describe a number of scenarios and apply a boundary focus to them, which then may guide the way to a solution. As you'll see, the implications are profound, and although you may have previously accepted you can't control anything outside yourself, you may sometimes find it difficult to stick with that conclusion. However, unless you want to continue going back and forth between one confusing situation and the next, prepare to tolerate these difficulties. Take my word: ultimately you make it easier for yourself.

Respect for boundaries

My right to act as I wish has one boundary: it stops at the tip of your nose.

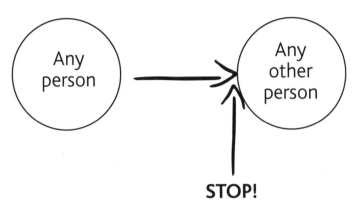

I have to respect my own boundaries as much as I have to respect yours, and vice versa. My reaction to your actions does *not* comprise my right to demand you change what you've done, said, or otherwise expressed, if done in a non-violent way. (Otherwise it's an assault and I have to protect myself.) My demand for your apology implies my opinion is correct, and you're wrong, based on my judgment.

I'm not referring to the *Can I get some respect around here* or *I deserve respect* kind of respect. This is the *What right do I have to demand that you're different from who you are just to please me?* variety of respect.

While we may be inclined to accept boundaries as a concept, the next hurdle is to have respect for their extent and content. Since these boundaries define a person, it implies having respect for everything that person values, thinks, says, does or feels. Unfortunately that's often quite different from what we want them to think, feel, say, do or value.

Of course, that respect doesn't equate to condoning or agreeing with everything people say or do. I still have the right to strongly, but respectfully, disagree. Call it the right to be stupid – but who's the judge?

Recognizing and respecting boundaries as the outer limits of another person's rights creates predictability. Although we may not necessarily like the nature of the boundaries and what they prevent us from doing, we inherently appreciate their existence. They allow us to relax. They determine what we can do, even when questioning or ultimately transgressing them, they provide our identification as 'law abiding' or 'outlaw', which without boundaries would not be possible. They may give us comfort in knowing we 'belong' to a particular group, or define our difference as to who we are in relation to others.

Respect = curiosity

When different opinions lead to an argument instead of a conversation, it's because we feel threatened, intimidated or scared by the other person disagreeing with us. We may feel the other person isn't taking us seriously or may even leave the relationship because of our differing opinion. In any case, we find it difficult, if not impossible, to respect the other person's right to their opinion.

At the same time we demand exactly that for ourselves, namely that our opinion is respected if not totally accepted. We not only want to be listened to, we also want the other person to give up their opinion for the benefit of our much more acceptable and reasonable one. This demand may come with attitude — *How dare you argue with me!* To make matters worse, we then become frustrated when the gratitude we expect in return for helping them change their minds is not forthcoming.

Here's a different suggestion. What if we treated the other person and their opinion with curiosity and the kind of respect we reserve for people with different backgrounds and experiences? We could then listen without reference to our dissenting opinions. After all, ours is just another opinion. If we stopped taking ourselves so seriously, we could listen and settle on *That's an interesting point of view* instead of feeling threatened by it.

Even if the opinion is directed against us, as in 'you're a right royal idiot', you can simply accept it as a captivating point of view, leaving it with the other person and not taking it on board. It may not always be easy, but it's possible if you remind yourself that it's only someone's opinion, to which they are entitled.

You can, of course, buy into the argument; but remember that in doing so you're choosing to allow the other person's opinion to enter your mind. You've started renting out space in your head to them.

In this diagram a relationship is symbolized by the overlap of the two circles, the common space — this signifies the reason we're engaging with this person.

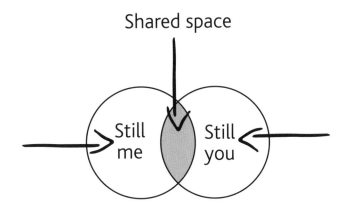

In disagreements we tend to focus more on our own expectations. Instead, appreciating what makes the other person different and unique can be a reminder of why you were attracted to them and therefore, made the effort to discover or create that common space, despite your respective differences. The acknowledgement of these differences is reflected in the respect you show the person.

7. **Common misconceptions**

As an introduction to common misconceptions and boundary violations, let me use the history of psychology as an illustrative example. From Papa Freud, to the behaviourists, cognitivists, humanists and many that followed with good ideas, they were all wrong as much as they were right. *Right* as long as they stayed within the defined boundaries of their investigations, *wrong* when they generalized their small area of exploration to the whole array of the much more complicated human behaviour, and transgressed and violated their boundary.

Generalizations

Generalizations about people often lead to boundary violations. This takes place every time we fail to respectfully treat a person as unique, and instead as a member of a group we assign them to. While it may be accurate to see someone as being typically American, Australian or any other nationality, it's also true that the person belongs to a number of other different groups. They would also be male or female, religious or non-religious, a parent, a single person or identify with a particular orientation. In other words, everyone belongs to a range of groups, classes and organizations. Why single out a particular trait? We do it at random, because it fits our own view of the world; in our minds we group people together in order to impose some kind of predictability.

It's also the price for the brain's increased sophistication. While it has been able to process increasingly more information as it developed over the millennia, it does so by sacrificing its attention to detail. It initially bundles information and applies a broad filter. This is more efficient than attending to all the small differences that separate individuals. As a person becomes more important to us we start to differentiate to a finer degree; but doing so with every person we meet would be a gross waste of energy as far as the brain is concerned, since we meet many people only once or twice, or they have no particular relevance in our lives.

Being mindful of boundaries and generalizations

Being aware of the brain's tendency to categorize in this way can help stop you from generalizing. Just because someone doesn't follow my religion, for example, doesn't mean she also has other attributes I may not like. Conversely, just because someone belongs to the same association doesn't make them a friend. Most importantly, just because someone is a friend — or partner — doesn't mean they have to agree with everything you do or say. When they don't agree with you it doesn't make them an enemy, either. It simply means they are an individual with their own opinion.

Manipulation

We describe someone as manipulative when they try to get their way, in a non-violent way, and come up against some form of resistance. The word conjures up the image of an evil, Machiavellian-style individual who uses others to meet their own version of what the world should look like.

Manipulation, however, is something we all do. Why do we tell jokes? To make the other person laugh for the same reason you find it funny. When you tell a sad story, when you tell any story, you really want the other person to agree with your sentiments. Unless you ask a question — and even then it's likely you've already made up your mind and know what you want to hear. If this doesn't happen, you try to convince them by your arguments. If this isn't manipulation, what is?

Once again we're very discerning when it comes to others, but less so when it concerns the things we do ourselves. Of course, there is a difference (isn't there always?): we don't do it with malicious intent. We call it *convincing* someone, a much nicer word. Manipulation is only what others do.

But what difference does this terminology make? In our own mind it may appease our conscience but in effect the outcome is the same. We try to bend someone to our own image and if they do not want to come around to our point of view there will be consequences. On important issues we may feel let down, unsupported, even betrayed. We may then terminate a friendship, tell others how weird that person is, or make some snide remark at the next opportunity.

But let me reassure you, this isn't the time to throw stones, because we're all sitting in the same glasshouse. The next time you feel you've been 'bent' because of someone else's behaviour, remember this is because *you* have allowed them to cross your boundaries. Instead of accusing them of manipulation you could accept responsibility for having allowed yourself to be manipulated.

In such circumstances, allow the other person to say what they like and then take responsibility for what it evokes in you, *and control that feeling*. No need for blame; simply accept responsibility for yourself.

Sweet expectations — rude awakenings

When we experience discomfort or 'dis-stress' in the absence of a clear and present danger, the feeling is usually associated with an event that doesn't meet our expectations, when reality fails to comply with our plans. Or we may worry about someone we care about or fear that a confrontation or some other unpleasant event is about to occur. We may expect something to occur but fate may decide otherwise. In any case, it's something external to ourselves.

A baby learns by observation, and then copies and repeats. In copying, the child is testing that the same outcome it previously observed will happen next time round. Repeating it afterwards is then based on the expectation that this outcome is stable and the realisation that *this is how it works*. We don't question this first 'knowledge' or implicit memory, as it forms the basis for our subsequent experience and interpretation of the world, and also shapes what we then regard as our 'values'. In computer terms, it configures our very own individual 'operating system'.

Our primitive brain is also wired for predictability and is therefore highly interested in creating facts and foreseeable outcomes, results that can be relied upon, and the basis for what we call expectations.

The problem with these expectations is that from now on we can only lose. If our expectations are met, nothing much has happened, because we already anticipated this outcome and made our plans accordingly — things simply turned out as expected. We generally only notice when things *don't* happen as planned. The result: despair, disappointment, frustration, loss of friendships, relationships, money, you name it.

The closer we are to someone, the higher our expectations, simply because we know them and how they'll react (or think we do). If our expectations aren't met it's not just disappointment that takes effect — the unpredictability of their behaviour is unsettling, given that we *expected* a certain behaviour. In holding such expectations about an outcome we've forgotten boundaries; we've forgotten where we end and the other person starts. We need to remember we can't 'make' another person respond in any particular way to our actions — and therefore can't expect to accurately predict the outcome or form an accurate expectation about that outcome.

As we've seen in Part 1, unpredictability causes discomfort on a very deep, subconscious level. By bringing it into awareness and giving it a name — disappointment — we elevate the unpredictability factor into the realm of what we can now accept as a 'fact of life', namely that people disappoint. We're making it almost *predictable*. Now that we have an explanation, we feel better, less stressed, since we can attribute our discomfort to a predictable factor, and another person and their fallibility. This is now a concrete identity we can accept, attack as immoral, forgive, or do with it whatever makes us feel better.

As important as expectations are for our system to be able to relax and feel at ease based on the assumption that behaviour is predictable, the possibility is inherent that they fail to materialize — and the effect of that failure is very unsettling. But if unpredictability is so damaging for our system, yet life is so altogether unpredictable, why aren't we all stressed to the max every single day?

While it appears that modern life is a lot more complex than that of our ancestors (or so we're inclined to believe), this isn't to say modern stressors are necessarily more significant. The poor old limbic system is quite a dumb 'relay station', and treats incoming information not only according to the threat it could pose but also as an isolated event. If too many things happen at the same time and demand a response it can be overwhelmed, and as a result we feel stressed.

However, when we developed a sense of danger we also developed the ability to accept stressors as a fact of life, which we now call resilience. It's built into our system and is part of our mental survival kit. Only when this ability is stretched and approaches its limits do we experience our circumstances as stressful.

Advice — and other donations

The worst vice is advice.

Al Pacino, *The Devil's Advocate*

When we're asked for something, anything really, we assume it's needed. So when we're asked for advice we often expect it will be followed. When I give advice I expect something in return, namely that you respect and validate my efforts, and are grateful for my wisdom — or something along those lines. It sounds fair enough, but is it?

Imagine an old man in the street, holding out his cupped hand, by inference asking for some coins. You feel generous and hand him twenty dollars. As you walk away, you turn around and see him disappear to invest your money in a high percentage return, 40-percent proof alcohol to be exact. How would you feel? What would you say? 'That's the last time you ever get anything out of me!' No doubt followed by a stern look and a disapproving frown.

He asked and you gave, and that should be the end of that. In fact, because there are no 'shoulds' as we will see a little further on, it's the end of the transaction. That's where your boundary ends. If you wanted to make sure how he was going to spend the money, you could have told him. If he were hungry, you could have taken him to the nearest hamburger stand or restaurant, let him place his order, paid and left.

When you give, do so unconditionally, otherwise ensure your conditions are well expressed and just as well understood. The same principle applies as when you cross boundaries: you take a risk. Once you donate something it's someone else's property — or problem. Any further expectation crosses the line between what was yours and is now theirs.

If you give something away, be it advice or material goods, you have no more right to it than if you sold it. That's the nature of giving. In return you receive the warm feeling of having shared your own good fortune. You can't ask for royalties — if you want that, write a hit song. Draw clear boundaries between what's freely given and what's conditional and comes at a price.

Luck — another boundary violation

The notion of good or bad luck comes in many guises, and isn't always overt. Dig a little and you'll find many lives are run by a belief in luck, or the lack of it. While it may exist in a parallel universe, in our cognitive world dictated by logic there's no place for such a thing. The belief in luck represents another violation of boundaries.

The belief in cause and effect is based on experience and seems to tell us that if I do x then y occurs. If this was indeed always the case, and the only variable involved, we could rightly assume that y happens when we do x. But wait, there's more . . . to life and to outcomes.

Would everybody connect the dots below in the same way? We make our own connections based on our experiences, expectations and predictions.

You could argue that life is a series of unrelated events, and we connect them as we please — and at our peril, because when things don't turn out as expected we become stressed.

While I don't want to end up becoming too philosophical, it's worth remembering that we construct our own reality out of morsels of information *of our own choosing*. Otherwise there could be no such thing as a surprise, since everybody would function and interpret the world in the same way. Like clockwork or, rather, *A Clockwork Orange*. In case you were too young to see it, this was a movie based on the novel by Anthony Burgess, in which the protagonist is subjected to mind-altering manipulation to conform to societal norms of non-violent behaviour.

When you buy a lottery ticket and miss out by one digit, does this mean the next time you'll win? Don't waste your money finding out. Missing out by one digit in a lottery draw does *not* guarantee you a win in the next, because each lottery draw is totally independent from any other.

When we talk about bad luck, or good luck for that matter, we pick some event — for which there may be a reason — and relate it to another — for which there may be no reason (rational connection) — and determine it was good or bad luck. Of course, you would justify your conclusion and claim these events weren't picked at random but relate to each other naturally.

If this was the case, everyone would have to come to the same conclusion. Even if you subscribe to a deterministic view of the world, where all the dots are connected in a predetermined way, we still don't know exactly how the connections run. It really doesn't seem to make any difference if free will exists or the world is predetermined but we don't know how.

And what about undertakers, car repairers, property maintenance people, in fact anybody in the repair business — wouldn't they consider your bad luck their good luck? The more bad luck you have, the more they thrive. Now that doesn't seem right!

Maybe — but only because the notion of bad or good luck is misplaced or, at best, quite useless.

Boundaries to the rescue!

Treat each event in isolation and you can easily see them related to many facets. Then it's just a matter of personal choice to view them as good or bad, or better still, to accept them as just an event that you deal with the best way you can. Often you may find that what you originally deemed good or bad turned into the opposite after some time had passed and other events took place. Then we often call it a stroke of good fortune, or a silver lining.

But how can that be? If it was good or bad, how can the same event all of a sudden be the opposite? The answer is simple: because it was never one or the other. It was always what we saw it as, *and then we changed our mind* when it suited. Not a matter of *being* blessed, rather a matter of *feeling* blessed. And feelings can change very quickly.

Ultimately, relying on luck is simply another way of creating predictability where uncertainty or confusion ruled. This same need is also reflected in superstition. If we can't find an explanation, we resort to the black cat, walking under a ladder, Friday the 13th and all the other superstitious no-no rules we've come up with over time. Being able to attribute a cause to an event makes us feel that little bit better. It gives us the illusion of some control over events — by avoiding it in the future we also avoid bad luck.

Your opinion of another person

This isn't strictly a misconception, but a frequent misinterpretation and overlooked key to unlock the secrets people try to hide.

When you make a statement about someone, it says nothing about them and everything about you.

Huh? How so?

When you observe what someone does or says, it triggers a response in you according to your experiences, values and expectations (your implicit memories or operating systems).

Any statement you make about someone else's behaviour simply reflects these expectations, and defines the difference between their actions and your expectations. It says nothing about their values . . . but everything about yours. Any opinion about them is a projection of what is going on in your own mind and says nothing about them at all. Instead it simply defines how you see and compare them to your own fantasies. The same applies when someone says something about you: their comments merely reflect their own expectations and thinking.

The following may help you not to be upset by what someone says about you, and that includes the people closest to you. When researchers showed people photographs of faces and provided a few details about their owners, the respondents determined within sixty seconds if they liked or disliked the individuals behind the faces. They decided if they were innocent or guilty of a crime, if they thought they were trustworthy, and made judgments about their personality that were nothing short of psychic, given the few details with which they had been provided.

This shows we form an opinion about a person within less than a minute after first meeting them. Obviously we don't much care if it's correct, or about details. Scary! How can we possibly make a judgment on someone based on such limited information? Here comes a much scarier thought (apart from having to face a jury that relies on a sixty-second assessment).

While our brain has achieved higher levels of functioning this has come at a price: quantity over quality. While we're able to take in a high amount of information, most of it is processed on a superficial level only — remember how I talked earlier about the brain's predisposition for efficiency?

The reason for this comes back to the brain's primary goal: keeping us safe and ensuring our survival. Being able to complete ever more complex tasks has resulted in a greater capacity to take in and process new incoming information, but also to put it in different contexts and use it in novel ways.

For example, we're now able to invent things to make our lives easier and can extract more information. This has resulted in a greater number and variety of neural networks, and the increased connectivity between networks has created highly complex activation sequences, which researchers are now trying to untangle and trace back to their origins.

The price for this higher processing power is the loss of attention to detail. In essence, we rely on less information to make more inferences. We call it pigeonholing and the advantage is that we don't have to spend a lot of time to make up our mind about a person. As far as the brain is concerned, that makes a lot of sense, since on this level of information processing, it's not interested in justice or fairness. So what if I make a wrong decision? To which the brain would argue: *Would you rather be safe or fair?* Ouch!

Incidentally, this consolidation of information happens on an almost daily basis. Think of your school years as an example. For most people school was a mixed experience, with both good and bad memories. Yet when asked, most people rate it either positive or negative, ignoring the details. How come? Because unless there is a very specific reason to dig deeper into our memory bank, that's good enough and the overriding impression will do.

We also do it with people. We rate them according to our opinion about them, as friends, acquaintances or people we don't want to know. Do these people have no redeeming qualities? Conversely, do our friends have no faults? We could hardly say that, and yet for us they are good people because we often ignore their negative (or what others may view as such) traits and base our relationship with them on rather selective criteria. These of course, also form the basis for expectations — and disappointments — as we've seen earlier.

When we pigeonhole, the (old, primitive) brain makes the decision for us and errs on the side of caution. The notion of fairness and justice originates in quite a different, and much more recent, part of the brain as the result of a subsequent 'higher function' analysis and is not essential for survival. In fact, it can result in the opposite. How many times have you felt disappointed by a foe, and how often by a friend? *Should have been more careful*, the old brain would say.

That's the reason the brain makes what we may call rash decisions, rather than well-considered judgments. The result of this is what I mentioned earlier: when we make a judgment about someone else, we really disclose more about ourselves than the person we're judging.

Scary as it may be, we can hardly escape that fact. Even when we *know* a person, we only know the picture we've constructed in our own mind about them, based on how they behave, compared with other experiences in our lives and cross-checked against their actions. The expectations we form of others are shaped by the opinions we hold. When they aren't met, and we feel disappointed, we blame them, whether they are classified as friend or foe. But for what? For not conforming to our expectations? While we may accept or expect nonconformity from our enemies, when this comes from our friends we react with disappointment.

Remember your boundaries before you speak

When we attach a label to someone after knowing them for a period of time, we reveal our own life experiences and the expectations they have fostered in us. Positive or negative, we give away what is or isn't important to us. Remembering where our own boundaries stop can remind us that what we say about others gives away much about ourselves rather than the person to whom our comments are directed. This should help us to be more mindful when we speak.

8. 'Self' containing boundaries

If you feel something is devastating, it's devastating for you no matter what anyone else says. No one can make you feel any different, unless you allow it to happen. Likewise, if something is all right by you, I can talk till the day is old telling you otherwise, and it will still be all right by you.

Everything is only as difficult, tragic, comfortable, unpleasant or whatever else you want to put here, as you make it.

If you can accept and apply this simple truth, it will change the way you react to life's events and the people who cause them. The challenge is to accept that events are just that — occurrences of neutral value, to which *you* assign a particular meaning. The nature of that meaning is your individual decision and this will differ from one person to another.

Exploring these ideas, and highlighting how a boundary focus can help free us from the restrictions we often place on ourselves through our emotional responses, is the aim of this chapter.

A *normal* response

Surely, you might think, if something bad happens it's normal to feel sad, angry or devastated? I don't dispute that certain reactions are normal and most people would react that way. What I suggest is that we don't *have to* react in the manner expected of us.

Many reactions we call *normal* are the product of what, to use a computer analogy, has been programmed into our operating system during infancy and early childhood. As adults, though, we're able to draw a boundary around the event and our reaction, rather than accept a particular reaction without question. We need to ask ourselves: *Can I learn to accept a situation without the negative associations and feelings that otherwise accompany my reaction to it?*

Drawing a boundary between an event and your reaction can be a truly liberating experience. It sets you free to make your own decision as to how you deal with a situation, rather than conforming to an expectation. When you stop and think about it, these expectations may or may not even be ones you truly agree with.

Let me use a provocative example: you find out your partner has cheated on you. The *normal* reaction ranges from disgust to disappointment and anything in between, but in any case brings up the issue of separation. Adultery is a cause for separation. Or is it?

I know better than to put my foot in it by simply suggesting that's your decision. I dare say, though, there's nothing to say you have to follow a particular course of behaviour without question *because it's normal*, the only available option, or the law. While leaving may be your first reaction, when you isolate the issue (betrayal) and your reaction (whatever it may be) you might come to a different conclusion. Even if, once you've done this, you've decided you can't live with a cheating partner, at least you know this isn't a decision made on a whim and due to unbridled emotions, but instead a rational one.

Rational, because you're realistic and acknowledge what you're capable of, and what you're not. If living with someone who cheated on you is beyond your ability, so be it.

The upside to letting go of pre-programmed responses is that it hands you back control over your reaction. While that may not always make you feel good, it will make you feel better than you would if you made an emotional decision.

In very emotionally challenging situations, such as the death of a child, grief can be overwhelming. In this situation your grief might be tempered by a choice to believe in an otherworldly higher power. A situation like this can be either devastating or the source of renewal and strength. Another way to try to create something positive from this situation is that you might choose to donate body organs, giving the chance of a new life for someone else. If we allow ourselves to make choices about how to react, we own the situation — rather than being dictated to by it.

The stress of *should*

If I had to name one theme, phrase or acknowledgment that comes up most often in therapy sessions I would have to say it's *I know, I should* . . .

This always reminds me of a friend who, in search of personal growth, returned from a workshop designed to help him in his endeavours (of course he was charged handsomely for it). He told me afterwards there is no such thing as should. This annoyed me no end, because at the time I damn well knew I *should* be losing weight, *should* be saving more money and *should* be trying to become a humbler person (I admit I'm still trying to lose weight).

So it's with a humbler mind I now concede he was right. It's not a helpful concept to say the very least. If there is such a thing as 'should' there shouldn't be.

When we say *should*, what we're really expressing is the fact that there are two worlds we live in: one is the wishful-thinking world, the other is reality as we see it. Our ideal hovers just somewhere above us, and we can't quite get there. But we feel we *should*.

This discrepancy between the real and the ideal of our imagination then causes the degree of discomfort we experience, a bad conscience or, you guessed it, stress. It's a demand placed on us (or one we place on ourselves), which we've either not been able — *or feel unable* — to meet.

How can boundaries help?

Whenever you say to yourself *I should*, follow it up by asking, *says who?* Is it someone else? Or is it you saying you should? If it's someone else, do you accept their authority? Obviously not, otherwise you *would* do as you *should*. (Note that if you're debating about something that is the law or a moral conviction, then it's not a matter of should; you'd better do it! Don't *should yourself* out of your responsibility.)

A boundary awareness puts *should* in the realm of wishful thinking, where it belongs rather than your everyday reality. Not recognizing it can truly spoil your day and leave you with a (permanent) guilty conscience.

If it's you who thinks you should, it doesn't mean you should, but that you *want* to. You can also say *I'd like to* or *Wouldn't it be nice?*, but rid yourself of the nagging *I should*. If you *want* to do something, do it. If you don't, leave it alone.

Experience the difference when you say to yourself *I want*

instead of *I should*. Just by saying this to yourself it may put you on a completely different, more direct mental path.

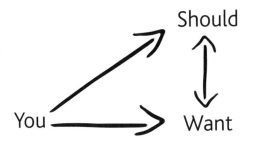

The degree of discrepancy between what we feel we *should* be doing and what we really want to do also determines the degree of our contentment.

Take the example of trying to stop smoking. Do you really *want* to stop, or do you think you *should*? Is it because you *should* be healthier and because people and your doctor told you so? Or do *you* really want to stop?

When you think I should you're looking for excuses; think I want and you'll be looking for ways and means to achieve it.

And why is such a small difference in the way you talk to yourself so important? Read on.

Oh, no, I'm talking to myself!

Does it mean you're losing it when you start talking to yourself? Think about the way you form an opinion. Do you talk to yourself, argue, weigh up the options, consider one side of the argument then the other, only to dismiss both and bring in another aspect? Do you sometimes find yourself in vigorous mental conflict when making up your mind? Many people may hesitate to agree, believing it would mean they're going crazy.

In fact, there's a much greater likelihood of there being something wrong with you if you don't talk to yourself. It's known as silent or inner speech and is the way we communicate with ourselves. Talking to yourself is normal, and the basis for the conclusion or opinion at which you finally arrive. Of course, the quality of this opinion depends on the quality of the conversation you're having with yourself. It's essential to monitor the input, your ideas and the way you talk to yourself, since it determines what you do and what comes out of your mouth. Ultimately, it also determines how you feel.

Deliberately guiding the path and direction of your thoughts ensures that what you do or say is also more carefully considered and less likely to be offensive or get you into unpleasant situations.

It's not so much a matter of think before you speak, but think about what you think before you speak.

The frequently cited Freudian slip is generally explained as the subconscious getting the better of you, where you reveal something you normally would prefer not to divulge. It would seem rather difficult to disprove such a theory, but to me such a slip only reveals your thought patterns. It's not subconscious at all. You're quite aware of what you're thinking. You may not necessarily have wanted to reveal it in company, and this is where the slip may come in, when you say what's *in* your mind, but not necessarily *on* your mind.

A further incentive to talk carefully with yourself may be the fact that the quality of this self-talk determines the quality of your opinion. Your attitude will be reflected in the way (and words) you think about something or someone, and will naturally spill into the way you express and share your opinion with others.

Naturally, that also applies to the person with whom you're having a conversation. The quality of that exchange is not only a reflection of the conversation you've had with yourself, it's also a reflection of the conversation the other person had with themselves. The better informed our self-talk the better formed our opinions and therefore the more productive the conversations we have with each other.

When you're confronted with what you consider an unacceptable or painfully ill-considered opinion, treat it as such. Rather than getting upset about someone else's ignorance (as you may perceive it) give the person the respect an ill-informed individual nonetheless deserves. It's absolutely vital that we 'talk to ourselves', but leave it there . . . it doesn't need to be revealed to the world. If you want to avoid unpleasantries being inadvertently revealed, as I said earlier, remember my advice:

Think *about what you want to think.*

Discrepancy — it can tear you apart

The conversations we have with ourselves also have implications pointing back to our infancy. We all experience things we don't like in childhood — and it's poor Mum again. (Wouldn't you know it!) This occurs because Mum either doesn't let us do what we want or forces us to do something we don't want to. In either case we feel less 'I love you, Mum', and closer instead to 'I hate you, Mum'. But what happens if a child expresses this feeling? Mum might respond by saying how sad that makes her feel. Alternatively, Mum may tell the child that in that case she may as well go away, in a *There's the fridge, help yourself* kind of manner. Either way, the child learns it's not such a good idea to express their true feelings, because they know they can't look after themselves, or because they don't want to see Mum sad.

This means that from now on the child has to learn to live with this discrepancy between what they feel on the inside and what they're allowed to convey. The child may be feeling one thing, but not be allowed to express it, or they may be encouraged to express a feeling they may not genuinely feel in a particular situation. The degree of this discrepancy is also the degree of discomfort we experience henceforth, and carry into and throughout adulthood.

The extent to which we were allowed to hold and express opposing feelings as children determines how, as adults, we'll be able to deal with the challenges relationships bring with them.

In order to minimise these internal discrepancies it's important we're truthful with ourselves in every respect, including self-talk. For example, if you think you're good at a particular task, acknowledge it at least to yourself and don't hold back. If you still have a way to go before you can call yourself proficient, don't fool yourself. It will be reflected in what you say and how you react towards others when you feel you're being criticized.

If you think one thing but say another you're bound to land in hot water at some stage. If not outwardly, you'll still feel the effects within yourself. The pain of feeling overlooked, chastising yourself that you *should have* said or done, or spoken up for yourself — whatever we sum up as regrets — can all be the result of dishonest self-talk. Call it *self-honesty* instead and reduce your unrealistic expectations and subsequent disappointment, in order to reduce the empty feeling when you *should have* done something, but didn't.

Guilt and regret — too much time on your hands?

Let's talk briefly about feelings of guilt. I leave out remorse here, although they all have a thing or two in common, but in my view the latter covers a different aspect of human behaviour. Regret and guilt relate to demands, which can come from both within and without, while remorse only covers my own expectations that I haven't fulfilled. Of course this distinction is open to different opinions.

All, however, have in common a retrospective approach to the here and now. Their relationship to boundaries is such that they transgress the boundary of time, often accompanied by a sleight of hand — well, *sleight of mind* to be precise.

When we regret an action, we apply what we know today to an action from a time when we didn't know what we do now. It's a variation of applying 20/20 vision to the past.

Does this make guilt and regret useless?

This depends on what we do with this guilt. Feeling guilty implies we've done something wrong or made a wrong decision. Yet, when you think back, didn't you do exactly what you wanted to do at the time based on the information you had? It's only now, with hindsight and after other aspects have come to light, that you go back in time and feel guilty. I find it difficult to believe you felt guilty at the time when you made the decision.

What a waste of time and energy! If you can show me that feeling guilty changes anything, feel free to give me a call and we can feel guilty together, if that's what it takes to make things better.

Feeling guilty can be useful if it leads you to make amends and thereby makes a difference in the here and now. Otherwise you can use your energy more productively. Draw a line around the events of the past and those of today. The present events are the ones you can decide to do differently. Feel guilty if you wish, but you can't change the past . . . not even with guilt.

Any feelings about the past are truly yours. Any embarrassment you may have suffered is in your own head. Nobody else will remember, unless you remind them. If they should remind you of past transgressions, feel pity and have mercy on them. Their life obviously isn't providing much for them if they have to hang on to the past and remember things that may have embarrassed you or where you may have done something wrong a long time ago.

Of course, this also applies to yourself. Forgiving and forgetting cuts both ways. If you find it difficult to forgive, yourself or others, try saying to yourself, *Everyone always does the best they can*, placing equal emphasis on each single word.

Nothing else makes any sense, unless you believe that someone would act against their own best (perceived) interest. While we don't always do what could universally be called 'the best', we still make the best decision as far as we're able to judge at the time.

That doesn't mean society has to always tolerate such behaviour. Of course, it has to protect itself against actions that threaten the wellbeing of others. It can detain people and sequester them, also known as locking them up, but that's quite different from feeling angry, wanting revenge or feeling guilty. It's to protect, not to punish. While the first is based on reason, the latter satisfies our thirst for revenge. Just observe what happens after a particular horrific crime has been committed. Unable to change what occurred, the first call is to increase the punishment provided by the law. Something previously seen as adequate is now no more, because we *feel* differently about it.

Mistakes and other misnomers

The feeling of guilt and regret is often coupled with the notion of having made a mistake. But what exactly do we mean? That I wanted to do x and ended up doing z? In other words, doing something I didn't want to do, by mistake?

As in the above cases that cause guilt and regret, we did exactly what we wanted to do, again using hindsight and knowledge gained after the event to now call it a *mistake*, sometimes also disguised as the *wrong decision*.

If we could only be more honest! We made the best decision we could under the circumstances, with what we knew or could know. If it turns out unfavourably, it's because something happened we didn't know or couldn't have known. So, why call it a mistake?

The answer in many cases is that we've not taken into account the fact we explored earlier, that we can't always affect the outcome of our actions. We've not been mindful of our own boundaries, and have compared our intention with the outcome. Trying to achieve something that turns out differently isn't a mistake — it's called life.

It's what happens while we make other plans. You could also explain it with the brain's disposition to create predictability. If I can attribute something unpleasant to a mistake I made, I have an explanation for the unforeseen outcome. Simply explaining it as *life* can be unsettling, since it reinforces the reality that life is unpredictable — which means it's threatening.

If you realize you made a rash decision, didn't inform yourself properly, or identify any other shortcoming prior to making a decision, *learn from it*. Calling it a mistake and coming down hard on yourself won't change anything for the better. If anything, it can only make things worse for you. As I explained, the quality and nature of your self-talk determines how you feel about yourself and how you'll approach a new situation. If it's laden with reproach you may want to prove something next time round, rather than dealing with the situation on its merits.

So, how about taking the view that from now on there are no mistakes, only learning opportunities? Try it. I think you'll find it makes a big difference.

Emotional boundaries — the not so cut and paste nature of emotions

Boundaries can mean the difference between emotions being part of a meaningful human experience or a blabbering and convoluted mess. While the first inspires personal growth, the second stunts it.

Emotions are *not* the enemy; it's what we make of them, both as the sender and receiver, that makes them a possible menace. As the receiver we can only respond to what we perceive and what it evokes and provokes within us. This is at the root of the problem. If I was able to know exactly what another person feels and their reason for what they say or do, there'd be no misunderstanding. They would be getting what they are asking for, if I decided to give it to them.

Since we interpret what we hear according to our own view of the world, the state or mood we're in determines the way we react. If we feel *threatened* (always take that in the widest sense of its meaning) then we react based on our level of arousal.

As the sender of signals we seem to have an unspoken expectation that we'll be understood in exactly the way we meant. This is really short-selling yourself. Underlying the assumption is that you're an open book, easy to read and easy to understand. Not so.

It would mean you don't see yourself as an individual, but someone who is transparent and a cut and paste version of a human being. Let me assure you: you're not! Your feelings and the way you express them are unique. If you can get only a fraction of your feelings across without being seriously misunderstood or causing offence, you're doing well.

Expect to be misunderstood when feelings enter the equation. In fact, if someone says 'I know how you feel' you can honestly reply 'No, you don't'. All we can aspire to do is to get close to understanding what someone else is feeling, since everybody experiences an emotion in their own personal way.

When expressing your emotions, if you expect misunderstandings you'll save yourself surprise or frustration. Recognize and respect the boundaries between you and everyone else . . . and accept the fact you're as unique as they are. Your emotions are for you to know and others to find out — just as theirs are for you.

9. **No boundaries —
the 'big' picture**

Let's have a look at how the misconceptions discussed in the previous chapter can lead to what are regarded as 'solutions', but often lead to more headache. Based on inherently flawed (wishful) thinking, they predetermine but also limit and confine what we consider to be options, or may blind us to the elephant in the room.

This chapter could equally be called 'In Defence of Free Speech', though this would imply a particular philosophical or political position. Instead, my intention is to arrive at a conclusion, which follows from applying a boundary focus irrespective of any ideologically flavoured stance that may support or contradict it.

Political correctness — how incorrect
Earlier we looked at the far-reaching consequences of accepting that nothing and nobody can make you do or feel anything, and how this simple truth reaches into the corners of daily life in ways you

may not have expected. Let's now look at a similar example: political correctness.

In a nutshell, political correctness demands you don't say, or do, anything I don't like. A reason often given is that those who can't protect themselves have to be protected. Particular feelings, perceptions and thoughts are projected by the 'protectors' onto others; the protectors assume certain feelings on the part of those they aim to protect if exposed to certain phrases, behaviours or treatment. This, in my opinion, seems to give them carte blanche to decide what is and isn't acceptable.

What does a boundary focus tell us?

Like everybody else, you have the right to speak up and propose a code of conduct if you wish — just as I have the right to ignore it and say what *you* may find politically incorrect.

Do what you like with it, deal with it, get over it, call your MP. But whatever you do, don't make your problem mine.

Sounds very much like *tough bikkies*? Let's see if a boundary focus leads us astray and turns us into mean, self-centred and prickly individuals, or if there's a valid reason to demand more self-responsibility on the part of those feeling aggrieved.

Political correctness cuts out my right to be inappropriate. But who decides what is and isn't appropriate? My joke may offend you, it may be crude, cruel or you may not find it funny. That will be up to you to decide based on your opinion — and therefore it's your problem. If you're in the majority you don't have to legislate because I'll be sidelined, isolated or 'outed' for what I say or how I say it. Being kicked out, I'll find myself alone or with people who share my sense of humour or viewpoint. This goes for religious fanatics as much as for political party-liners.

But what's really behind the call for political correctness? Has the baby been thrown out with the bathwater? The give-away is the word *political*. Since politics change with the need to attract votes, so do the rules of political correctness. If political correctness was indeed a matter of morals, it would also be immoral not to help and care for the needy, downtrodden, refugees, etc., as some people believe. Yet, when do the majority of us help? Often not when it's really needed, but at a time when the powers-that-be decide it would be beneficial to themselves. The ones who do help don't need any prompting. Just as they don't need to be prompted to be politically correct.

If I call you a big, fat ugly whale (and you may replace this with any other politically incorrect comment) you can have one of many reactions. For one, you might not recognize yourself in that description. In that case, why respond at all? You may also disagree and believe that big, fat whales are beautiful; we're all entitled to our opinion, and yours is as good as mine. The last option might be that you agree. In that case, why argue and tell me I can't state what seems to be an agreed fact? Ignore it or start to lose weight, but don't tell me what I can or cannot say.

As you can see, in none of these circumstances is it necessary for anyone else to become involved. Public consensus will convince me to toe the line, hold back, rephrase or keep my opinion to myself. If not, are we really so insecure that we're afraid one person's opinion will cause the fabric of a functioning society to collapse? If it's that fickle, no law or regulation can save it.

Respect and political correctness

The concept of boundaries often requires a re-think, and tests your tolerance. To hit me with my own stick you could now demand I temper my language in the name of respect. But that would be a misunderstanding of what *respect* stands for in a boundary-focused approach.

It's the respect you afford others, not demand for yourself, that's important here.

A *demand* leans on someone in order to make them do something they might not want to do or stop them from doing something they want to do. It curtails their freedom to express themselves, crosses into their territory and is a boundary violation. As long as you don't physically hurt me I have no right to demand anything of you, not even respect. If it's not given freely I can only respect your right to withhold respect.

Staying within my boundaries demands I deal with my frustration and respect everybody's right to be as offensive as they care to be. What I might find offensive is *my interpretation* after all, and may not be theirs. Think of a belief you hold that someone else doesn't recognize. Avoid whatever you might find offensive, but don't expect others to pander to your sensitivities. Think about religious fanatics in particular, who feel compelled to protect their god, prophet or other representative. Isn't it sacrilegious of them to believe they are bigger than their god, and that they have to protect him? I would think he can look very well after himself and doesn't need me to kill in his interest.

When I put it this strongly it's with the aim of finding the middle ground, which we can only do after we've first established the ground rules, boundaries which are defined by their extremes. If we all take responsibility for our own reactions, we can start talking to each other about how to make life more tolerable all around and meet somewhere in the middle. No need for law or regulation.

Take an extreme example, like the hate-speech of the Ku Klux Klan. While I don't like it, and don't agree with them, I would fight for their right to espouse their stupidity. Hate speech only runs in open doors. Like suicide, you can't talk someone into doing it if they haven't already considered it for themselves. Yes, it's a hard world. And when have we ever succeeded in killing off an idea by forbidding it?

By starting with the right premise there is a chance for real compromise, not one dictated from above, which is only likely to drive individuality into the underground. Tolerance has the potential to foster curiosity and lead to *asking* rather than *demanding*, and *convincing* rather than *forcing* my view down your throat.

However, there's another dimension to political correctness. It emasculates and reduces responsibility for our own actions, in what we do as much as in what we say. We needn't think for ourselves and decide what is and isn't appropriate; we're told what to think or do and then simply follow. It seems part of a wider trend to shepherd, if not shoehorn, people into one way of thinking. I'm not necessarily proposing it's part of a concerted conspiracy to brainwash everybody. It seems more the result of interest groups shoulder-charging through the back door, half-opened for a different purpose, to dump their ideas on an unsuspecting and unprepared audience.

In days gone by, *political correctness* was called tact, sensitivity, diplomacy, good judgment, and it was each individual's responsibility to execute their own interpretation. Some were on the fringe, others known to 'call a spade a spade', and the more extreme ways of expressing views were dealt with through public criticism, discussion and critique. Because it was also open to public scrutiny everyone could decide for themselves what was and what wasn't acceptable . . . to *them*.

Boundaries instead suggest that if you don't like it, deal with it. I'll say it again: don't try to make *your* problem someone else's. Treasure your own sensitivity and convictions, but don't expect others to hold them in the same esteem.

The chains of political correctness don't liberate and don't make the world a better place. They only curb the expression of what already exists and drive it underground. From there it'll eventually find its way to the surface, but who can tell how or when? Especially on the political level, legislating the expression of an attitude or opinion, undesirable as it may be, can only make it more intriguing and attractive to the undecided, rather than prevent them from agreeing and joining it.

Leave the bully alone — literally

When discussing bullying, I'm not talking about physical bullying, which isn't bullying but assault and a criminal offence. *Your* freedom to express *your* opinion stops at the tip of *my* nose. Say what you like, but don't touch!

> **It's not the perception of what other people think was said or done by a bully that's important, but what the victim perceives was intended.**

Remember that we discussed earlier how nobody can make you feel anything? Even if I wanted to bully you, if you don't see it as such and treat it as a joke or ignore it, there's nothing I can do about that. I may continue doing what I'm doing, but what would be the point if there is no effect?

Having dealt with individuals who felt they were bullied, I can confirm my sentiments were often challenged by both my compassion for the victim and also the possibility the alleged bully may not have had any idea they were perceived as such. Some, however, were well aware of their actions and defended or explained them as simply the expression of their opinion, their personality or just being forthright.

When asked to mediate, it was often a complicated situation of claims of bullying or cultural insensitivity countered by those of hypersensitivity, lack of a sense of humour, chip-on-the-shoulder, and so on. Complicated indeed, but does it need to be?

If I'm allowed to say whatever I like — in principle — and it's your responsibility to deal with the feelings this may evoke in you, and we draw clear boundaries of what is my responsibility and what is yours, the answer suddenly becomes quite simple.

In Part 1 we saw how the sensitivity of the amygdala is set at different levels for each of us, and determines what we perceive as a threat or laugh off as a joke, based on our individual experiences. Is it really my responsibility to take account of your experiences in childhood, or any time in your life, and the difficulties they've caused for you?

Sure, if I know you belong to a religious group I could be expected not to make jokes that would affect your sensitivity. But what if I consider your religious group a cult and feel my own beliefs are offended, even by your demand to respect what I find offensive, such as Sharia Law? What if you're a refugee, and instead of respecting your sensitivities I hold you responsible for the turmoil you're now escaping from? Troubling questions, indeed.

The question attains even greater relevance when put into a wider context, that of personal freedom versus individual affliction. Take the use of perfume. Is it reasonable to request I don't wear perfume in public because someone may develop an allergic reaction to it? If you think this is far-fetched, this was exactly what was proposed for the New York subways.

As a result of overzealous legislation we're not used to assuming responsibility for our actions anymore. Yet when the law is unable to further regulate and make decisions, usually when it starts to cost money, we're suddenly confronted with the by now unfamiliar task of having to resume responsibility for ourselves.

It seems to me we often confuse the unfamiliarity of this feeling of personal responsibility with the substance of what we oppose. We don't really oppose the freedom of speech, rather the fact that we can't stop someone else enjoying that very right.

To test this, imagine being accused of bullying for having simply said what you think you're entitled to say. How would you feel about being told to stop being yourself? It would make perfect sense that if you don't like something, you walk away. If you don't like colleagues talking about you and you can't deal with it emotionally, seek help to develop coping strategies or change jobs. Bullied over the internet? Use the 'off' button. It's the same as the 'on' button and you know where that is.

Boundaries and expression of opinion

Think of the many possible sensitivities people could expect you to be aware of and accommodate. I might not know about your religious convictions and keep making comments that are offensive to you. I might not know you can't tolerate criticism because of experiences that have left you scarred for life. I might not know about your sexual preferences and keep making inappropriate references.

A boundary focus suggests you don't rely on the other person to stop doing what they are entitled to, namely expressing their opinion, even if you or possibly the majority of people don't like it. The expectation when you use a boundary focus is simply that you deal with it or walk away.

Education about boundaries would commence in childhood. Take the case of a child being excluded by other children. Well-meaning adults interfere. Instead of teaching the child to find their own way to fit in with the others and become accepted, adults take away that responsibility. Now the 'bullied' child never learns how to fit in with others, and the other children fail to develop their own sense of fairness. Instead, the mechanisms that led to the exclusion of the child are driven into the underground and hidden beneath the label 'bullying', to no one's benefit.

All such bullying, be it in the playground, school or workplace, could instead be a learning opportunity for the bullies as much as for the victim. It's simply human behaviour we've arbitrarily hung a label on — nothing more, nothing less.

It would sort itself out fairly quickly if it was deemed unacceptable by everyone and people would indeed be offended by it. The ultimate response would be a kind of exclusion or ostracism of the bully. Not to teach him a lesson, nor to get him to change his behaviour. That's his own choice, and he may choose to be avoided by others or, conversely, take the hint and find out why everyone shuns him and learn something in the process.

Here I need to point out that I am not proposing a solution, merely reminding you of the facts. How you implement them is up to you. In practice, bullying can be complex, especially if the bully is admired by his peer group and regarded as one of the cool kids.

What I am saying is just don't violate boundaries. It can only lead to further problems. If physical assault is involved, then call the cops! In cases not involving violence, for instance cyber-bullying, you work with both, but foremost with the 'victim'. Otherwise you only move the problem on to them, and the next time it happens they have no tools with which to deal with the situation — and possibly no one to help them this time.

In other words, we can leave the bully alone — literally — and thereby make it clear we don't condone their behaviour. No need to interfere and write reams of policies that are as useful in stopping bullying as they are in stopping grass growing.

The benefit of leaving the bully alone is that the victim is no longer disempowered by a focus on the bully. If we could genuinely succeed in protecting the victim, we would really be confirming to them that they are 'victims' who need to be protected and need someone to act on their behalf, because they can't look after themselves. How condescending!

A boundary focus tells us that if someone feels victimized no one can stop them feeling this way but themselves. Even helping them try to resolve the situation can result in them feeling victimized — again. We established earlier that we can't control someone's feelings, so ultimately it's up to the individual to find a way to come to terms with their perceptions. Why not put that at the start rather than the end of the process?

When leaving it to the victim to act for themselves right from the start, they are empowered and also encouraged to act without becoming a bully themselves. They are no longer reliant on people listening to them, believing them and taking action against the bully *for* them. They can decide themselves that the bully holds no sway over them, if they don't allow it to happen.

After the bully has been told about the inappropriateness of their behaviour and the consequences have been outlined, they may decide to keep their distance from the victim and keep to themselves. Ultimately, there's always the option of totally sidelining 'bullies', while at the same time it's not for who they are, but how they behave.

Ostracizing the bully is one example of how to deal with real or perceived bullying, and allows the person the opportunity to change their behaviour and then rejoin the group if they wish. If not, there is no harm done, and everybody goes about their business in their own way.

Mental disorder — illness or blessing in disguise?

Boundary theory casts a long shadow and allows, if not forces, us to view the world through a different lens, never more so than when considering what we define as illness or a disorder.

In our group practice, a very rough estimate would put the number of clients coming in for treatment of depression and/or anxiety easily at 50 per cent, and probably closer to 80 per cent. Asking gently about what occurred before depression struck, how they rated their family and love life, their relationships and work–life balance often reveals that their inner alarm system had been ringing for quite some time. There was the infection or flu that wouldn't go away. Friends were pointing out 'you're not the same', expressing their concerns in questions like 'Are you OK?'. They found it difficult to fall asleep, and when they eventually did, woke in a sweat soon after, before lying awake for hours again.

In short, their stories often reveal many indicators and valiant attempts about how they tried to deal with initially quite simple issues, which turned increasingly into more complex issues until it all became too much. They then mustered enough courage to confront their situation, or their partner urged them to seek help. Almost a success story — but sadly many others end up in an emergency ward after attempting suicide, or in the worst case, succeed in their attempt.

At that point, but unfortunately also only in retrospect, the signs are easily identified. The people close to the sufferers recognized the gradual deterioration, but at the time attributed it to other causes. Sometimes the straw that broke the camel's back is identified and the puzzle is solved.

While I may agree with the straw, my conclusion differs. Rather than focusing on the nature of that straw, I suggest it is its position that did the damage. That same straw at the beginning of this journey to depression may not have presented a problem at all. Only when it was on top of everything else did it break the camel's back, as the saying goes. If the signs were there, why did nobody see, read and understand them at the time?

Well, for one, because we don't know what we don't know. If depression strikes for the first time, we often don't know the signs, so how can we recognize them? The best advice I can suggest here is to contact a mental health professional if you're concerned about yourself or someone close to you. It can never be too early, but can often be unnecessarily late. There is nothing to be afraid of when asking for help. The worst that could happen is the doctor tells you 'No, you're not depressed'. Actually, that's good news — I can certainly think of worse results. Even if it's suggested that you might be depressed, at least you can then seek further help to prevent the illness from progressing, which is still a positive outcome.

However, this attitude toward mental affliction isn't specific to depression, but valid for what we generally call illness or disorder, which seems to be synonymous with 'dysfunctional'. I suggest it's far from it and instead a very *functional* reaction the brain initiated in response to what it perceives as a threatening situation.

What happens when we become depressed? We become listless, unmotivated, find fewer and fewer activities enjoyable and become increasingly less involved in matters that concern others and ultimately ourselves. Essentially we retreat from the world, because we can't meet the demands and the expectations, including our own, we feel are placed on us. We stop taking care of things and ourselves. It all piles up, creating a new set of problems to which we feel unable to attend. The result is that someone else has to take over, so we can take the time to recover. What's dysfunctional about that? Isn't this a very logical chain of events?

Rather than trying to fix the symptoms (the obvious unhappiness), it seems more logical to address the underlying causes. Changing the bandage to stop the bleeding doesn't get rid of the thorn that's causing it. The concept of boundaries allows for recognizing depression and many of the other mood disorders as a symptom, not an illness. I'll talk about this in more detail later on, when I apply a boundary focus to clinical issues.

Getting involved

Getting involved can be fraught with the risk of frustration for individuals as much as for governments and other organizations. This makes a boundary focus so pertinent, since it's universally applicable and relevant to both. Every time we become involved with trying to solve someone else's problem, others — and often many more — are created as a result. That goes for interpersonal situations as much as it does for any level of government.

Take, for example, the criminalization of drug taking. This has put a strain on society in many ways. The financial and human resources used to police and prosecute offenders are consequently not available for health care, infrastructure and the education system. Yet has drug taking been reduced? It would seem not.

This underscores the relevance of a boundary focus and the danger of 'getting involved'. If drug taking is a problem, it's not solved by imposing criminal sanctions but by addressing the reasons for it. If I can't make a difference, why become involved in the first place? A boundary focus would answer that question before becoming entangled in futile involvements and unhelpful laws.

Having no control, as we've seen, leads to stress, which then finds its own release valve and we become anxious, angry or depressed. Now extend this concept to a problem your partner/child or friend has, let's say their 'unhappiness', but you can replace this with any other issue.

This is a variation and further consequence of what I discussed at the very beginning: the risks we take when we internalize something. If the other person has a problem, as in the diagram below, they can deal with it; it remains their issue.

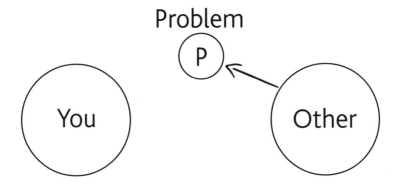

It's something you can take part in by talking about it with them, being a 'sounding board' and by discussing options and so forth.

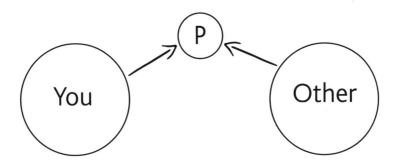

If they have internalized the problem, it now becomes a part of the person, and they become vulnerable, because now you don't talk about 'the problem' (an external issue) anymore; you talk about 'the person with that problem'. The person has become one with the problem, as the diagram overleaf shows:

If you attack the problem, they'll feel you *also* attack them. Hence, they may be reluctant to follow your advice, or may even become annoyed with you, despite your good intentions. They'll defend themselves, as we do when we feel attacked:

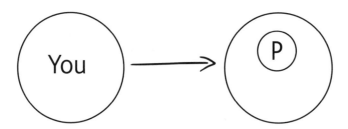

You may feel compelled to change the situation and make the person happy again, or somehow solve their problem, give advice or take some other action, because you can't tolerate seeing them suffer. Your intention is to deal with the problem, which you feel you have to solve and as a result you now internalize the problem, making it your own.

This is the first step to disaster, because you accept something as part of you which is not. And attached to that problem is another person.

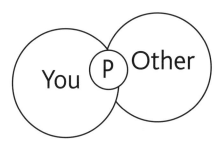

As you can see, it's now becoming increasingly complicated. Whose problem is it now? Since two individuals lay claim to the same issue, who has the right to the solution?

You've made an issue that wasn't yours in the first place your own. You now want/expect the other person to deal with it in the way *you* think most appropriate. Because we're all different, and therefore see the same problem from different perspectives, your solution may not satisfy the other person, and vice versa. But they have to act and you have no way of controlling what they'll do.

The problem is called stress. As you realize the situation is an unpredictable one over which you have no control, you may resort to ever more desperate means, which only makes the problem worse or creates new problems.

I believe the answer to this situation is to respect the other person's right to their problem *and their right to solve it their way*. This includes their right to make (even costly) mistakes as far as you're concerned, but nonetheless, let them do whatever they need to do. If it lands them in the same trouble as last time (which you wanted to avoid), because they just don't seem to learn, it's ultimately THEIR problem and their right to make mistakes — if you insist on calling it that. You may call it a mistake; for them it might be a solution. Different words based on different perspectives for the same outcome.

If you *respect* this entitlement and regard it as *their* issue, it allows you to stand by, listen and ultimately possibly make a decision: *It's all yours, and I'm leaving you to it.* Most importantly, you can do this without running yourself into the ground, creating stress for yourself, and without any misgivings about your own shortcomings if your 'good advice' turns out to be anything but. Because it was never your problem, you could never be expected to come up with a solution.

In a previous incarnation I was working in construction and at times relied on a friend to give me a hand. He often had different ideas from mine about how to go about certain jobs, which made me feel unsure about my own ideas. At that time I hadn't yet developed a strong sense of boundaries. He then used to add what he thought was reassuring, but which I found really annoying: 'But you know what you're doing.' Which of course helped to make me feel just that little bit more unsure of myself.

However, I've now come to appreciate the power of this strategy. It allows you to say what you want to say, but at the same time absolves you from any responsibility. It lets you express your doubt, while at the same time expressing faith in the other person's ability.

10. **Relationships not battleships**

If I throw a ball at you, it's up to you to catch it. If you simply let it drop to the floor, you've decided this isn't your game and you're not getting involved. But if you catch it, we've got ourselves a game. You express an interest in the ball not going where it otherwise would. We now share a common interest in the ball. Except I might have aimed the ball at something else, and you simply interfered. Or I might have been bored and wanted to start a game.

It seems an apt description of a relationship. When we first become involved with someone, we don't really know their intentions. We may assume an underlying common interest, but even that may be from different positions. Think of lawyers for two warring parties. They too, have a common interest in a case, but from opposite perspectives. The same can apply to any relationship.

You may be looking for a person to love, and meet someone who's also looking for a partner. But his interest may be primarily determined by the wish to find a mother for his young children after a recent divorce, or because his wife has passed away. While *someone to love* is also important, it's for a different reason.

When we enter a relationship, be it as an intimate partner, spouse, even a business relationship, we've some areas where our individual interest becomes a shared one. Note how I said 'interest', not 'interests'. This is another cause for misunderstandings, as we'll see. Just because we share an interest in stamp collecting doesn't necessarily mean we're also suited as friends. In the following diagram, the shaded area symbolizes where our interest overlaps.

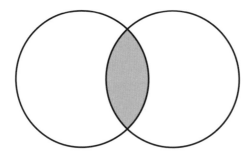

This overlap is also presumably the reason for the relationship, be it a personal one, a business partnership or membership of a club.

However, while in a drawing it's easy to identify the overlap and give it boundaries, in real life neither the exact position nor the content of these boundaries can be so precisely defined. One thing becomes clear in this drawing, which is often forgotten: beyond the shared shaded area, there remains a large portion of each person's individuality, personality or sacred space, the part that will forever be exclusively 'me' and, conversely, 'you'.

Some of it we may share over time, some we may choose to keep to ourselves. It may even be beyond our own grasp and we may not have access to this part that makes us who we are. It could be part of our implicit memory, and form the very basis of our subconscious belief system, the driving force for why and what we do.

These implicit memories begin to form when we first start learning about the world as a baby. As I explained earlier, from the first moment we communicate with the world, neural connections are formed and influence the way they interact with, and determine, subsequent connections. They lay down how neural pathways connect to new networks; this subconscious process shapes our perception and makes us unique in the way we use these implicit memories.

Just because two people love each other doesn't mean they now meld into each other. While in a very romantic and idealized version of love 'becoming one' is a favourite theme, I'm afraid the operative word here is *idealized*. As Kahlil Gibran put it: *Let there be spaces in your togetherness — the oak tree and cedar grow not in one another's shade.*

While I don't suggest giving up on striving for this unity, I would like to point to the ideal nature of it. Implicit in the notion of ideal is the fact that even though we may get close, we can never achieve it, lest it stops being an ideal. While the dictionary may define ideal in terms of perfection, philosophically 'ideal' means 'not achievable'. It's a theoretical 'idealized' state, once it's achieved it's not an ideal anymore — by definition.

Now for the overlap

It may be human nature that, as a relationship develops over time, partners start to extend the shaded area in the mistaken belief it represents a total congruence of the two circles (interest becoming interests), in other words neglecting the areas on each side of the overlap. As I pointed out, it's easy to define the overlap on paper as *this is what we share and have in common.* In real terms that assumption represents the essence of the difficulties within relationships.

We could call it taking liberties or it may simply be that, as we get to know and feel comfortable with each other, we extend the assumed common ground. Common ground, though, is often only in our own mind; we take it to mean we now have permission to intrude into the other person's space without it being perceived as an intrusion. After all, we're an item now, which often goes hand in hand with the presumption that the nature of the relationship allows us to take that step further, take a little more, expect a little more . . . or, conversely, presume you have to give or do a little less.

I often hear couples complain about this change in their partner's attitude not too long after their marriage vows have stopped reverberating through the wedding venue. Exploring different complaints may have led to the superficial wisdom that women tend to want to change their partner, while men want their partner to stay the same. (While undoubtedly superficial, many people seem to agree with this preposterous proposition.)

When I earlier referred to the testing of boundaries as human nature I excluded Tapsy, my late dog. Decidedly not human (despite having some very familiar traits), he seemed to have a pretty good sense of how to test what he was allowed to do and where he wanted to do it. So it may not be *human* nature after all, but rather a by-product of our evolutionary development. The higher up the ladder in the pecking order, the more we may feel entitled to privileges we assume come with that status, so this trait has now become *second*, rather than *human*, nature. It would support the contention of boundaries being an evolutionary need, gaining in importance as species develop social interactions on a higher level.

To illustrate the point take the following example. You decide to form a car pool with some colleagues and assemble daily at a meeting point. One day a colleague asks if you can pick him up from home, since his car is being repaired. You're happy to help. As it so happens his car then has to stay in the garage for some major repair and your one-off offer turns into a regular event. Before you know it, you're doing all the driving instead of sharing, because through all this you've formed a closer relationship and it doesn't seem like a big deal. But what if you have a falling out?

While you may not agree with this example, you probably agree with the idea that an innocuous proposition can result in a major commitment over time. While I'm not specifically talking about a one-night stand that lasts for twenty years, it may well have been subject to the same mechanism.

Yes, but . . .

Boundaries don't imply that individuals who use them are self-centred and egotistical. Instead it suggests you accept others as individuals and respect their right to be different. It also requires respect for the experiences that underlie and drive their different expectations.

In my example you may have noticed I made you the other person. And that means that as much as any person you meet deserves respect for their individual feelings and reactions, so do you.

That doesn't make you selfish or self-absorbed if you act accordingly. A boundary-focused relationship is built on this reality and any problem is resolved on the basis that you're responsible for your own feelings, and do *not* hold anybody else responsible. We respect, rather than attack each other for our differences.

If you find yourself in a convoluted situation either of a personal nature or involving a number of different issues, drawing boundaries around each issue gives you a new direction in which to proceed. Boundaries establish an undeniable truth and can act as an orientation point around which to reconstruct the relationship or issue. Boundaries are value neutral, but put a reality ring around unrealistic expectations and remind each party of their own limits and limitations. They re-establish personal space, a place where we're entitled to respect, if only for the existence of the boundary defining us as an individual. Separating individual issues or problems is the necessary first step to resolving them.

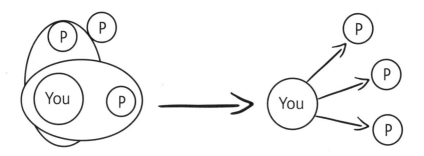

Play the ball, not the man

A client of mine explained to me he was sorry every time he lost it — that is, doing exactly what he didn't want to do. However, feeling sorry did little for his relationship, which eventually suffered as much from his outbursts as from his seemingly habitual apologies. So how do you get to the point where you *can* control the energy of your emotions without exploding, while at the same time respecting boundaries, yours and everyone else's?

As we've seen, we're more animal than we may want to admit, and primitive reactions often take precedence over thinking. But this is simply an interpretation of your actions after the event, not a valid excuse. I want to emphasise this difference between *explanation* and *excuse*, because they're often fatally mistaken for each other.

We react in a way that may seem to us instinctive, or how we think everyone in our situation would behave. And if your reaction was normal, everyone *would* react in that same way and it wouldn't be a problem for exactly that reason; it would be considered *normal*. However, if your reaction is a problem, it's not triggered by *what* you respond to, but instead because of the way *you* interpreted what you experienced.

Our first response to an event is to interpret what we see or hear. What we *do* as a result, our reaction, is really only our second response. Based on our perception, we then choose our action and sulk, scream, run away, lash out or whatever it may be. This physical action is based on the way we perceive what happens around us and is shaped by external influences as much as our previous experiences.

Whatever your boss, supervisor, friend or partner says or does occurs in a context, not in a vacuum. It's less *what* we actually hear or see, and more a question of *who* says or does it. Think of a stranger approaching you and calling you something you don't appreciate, let's say 'You moron'. Would you react the same way if your best friend called you that? Quite unlikely; you *may* get more upset if someone you know calls you that or you may treat it as joke, friendly banter or a term of endearment.

It becomes more complicated the more intimately you know a person, simply because there are more possible reasons for what they say or do. When we think about a stranger's action the question is simply: *Do I care?* When we question a friend's action it's more likely to be: *What are they trying to say?*

What your partner says or does is — almost automatically — imbued with extra meaning. It's this aspect that contributes to your reaction, and leads to arguments and discontent. In those situations we're not playing the ball, we're playing the man.

Playing the ball means you focus on the essence of what is said or done, not on the fact that *they of all people* said it. Maybe they were the only one who dared to speak up and say what you don't want to hear. Or it may be an ongoing, predictable and repetitive argument run on autopilot, regardless of its relevance.

In that situation, it may be especially helpful to think in terms of boundaries to be able to identify and isolate individual issues, and then stay with one issue, one feeling or one situation. Think of it as a to-do list. Would you start washing the car while you're making breakfast, but then stop to write a letter, only to return to washing the car while calling a friend as you quickly vacuum the carpet?

When you disagree and start to argue, make a rule: work on one issue at a time. That includes your feelings. Isolate them from the issue you're discussing. For example try: *When you say that, I feel like* . . . rather than: *You make me so angry when you say that.*

You can never be blamed for saying how you feel and why. Holding someone else responsible only takes you further away from a solution . . . and closer to a fresh argument.

If another person has control over the way you feel, they would also be able to control when your feelings change back again — so you would feel sad or angry until they changed your feelings. While often not overt, this thinking seems to underlie the stress we experience in a confrontation with a loved one. It feels as if they have the power over your feelings, and this perceived lack of control triggers your subconscious stress reaction.

Let me reiterate the good news: no one can make you sad or change your feelings. So if you don't want to, you'll never have to experience this helplessness again. When you approach a conflict, do it with a mindset that getting angry is *your* choice, not another person's doing.

You can allow yourself to make other choices or deny yourself that luxury. Indulge yourself!

How we choose our problems — sorry, partners!

Have you ever walked in a room, let's say at a party, and not known anyone? What's the first thing you do after you say a general 'hello' directed at nobody in particular and are left standing by yourself? Do you look around and search for the person you'd most like to meet or talk to? Do you look for someone who appears interesting or catches your eye?

I'm sure most of us will be able to relate to or recall such an experience. How come we're attracted to someone we've not even met yet? Let me symbolize a person in the following way:

To be attracted (and attractive) to that person you have to be similar in some corresponding way, since only a quality we're familiar with can have any meaning, and be either attractive or unattractive to us. Something we've no concept of is, in the first instance, meaningless. A person from Mars (let's just say, or from anywhere with a totally different physical layout) can't be physically or sexually enticing, because of a lack of familiarity.

When choosing a partner we look for what is familiar, for someone who is able to understand us, and by implication, our needs. We might *also* look for what is the opposite of how we see ourselves — because we've not been able or allowed to express that part of ourselves, but may find it very attractive in someone else. Since they're familiar in a way that allows the attraction to take effect, we sense our desires and needs can be met by that particular person.

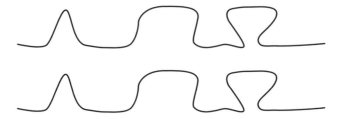

Being familiar means they would also have experienced, to some degree, similar needs and desires. They would know what we're looking for without having it explained. Sometimes this is referred to as a 'special someone', 'soul mate' or 'love at first sight'.

Now a number of things can happen. Despite sharing similar life experiences and interests and being familiar with our needs, due to our changing circumstances these could be shifted slightly, so that they don't occur in sync anymore.

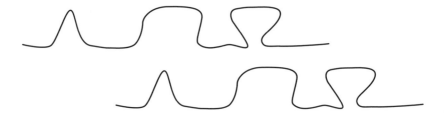

This creates tension and clashes with some other trait we may share, including traits we may not want to acknowledge, or even dislike, in ourselves. For example, we may not like our shyness, or the fact we're sometimes envious of others. To see it in the other person allows us to attack and criticize it. This is a much more attractive proposition, as it's easier to criticize something in someone else rather than in ourselves. We also feel better, because we now have the satisfaction of having chastised something very undesirable — even if only in someone else.

This now reinforces the dislike we have for our partner, who has this *really bad habit.* This is a great trick we can play to make ourselves feel better, if it wasn't for the ultimate price we often have to pay: a broken relationship.

What else can go wrong with the synchronization? Let's say that, as babies, we start off as perfect circles. As already discussed, mothers often forbid or remove that which a baby desires most, often in the interests of safety (grabbing a baby's hand before it touches the enticingly red-hot stove, for example).

When we add this perceived hurt, the circle is no longer perfect.

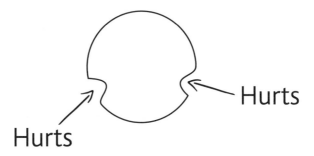

While Mum's reasons are exactly that, 'reasonable' and something her baby conspicuously lacks, the baby only knows how it feels when it's exposed to such experiences. And it hurts, especially the feeling that *Mum doesn't really love me, or else she wouldn't prevent me from doing what would make me soooo happy*. While this is due to the baby's very limited perception, based on feelings not reason, it's the only one that counts at the time and becomes stored in the baby's emotional memory. As a result it protects itself, to ensure these emotional wounds don't become aggravated.

When this occurs, and layers of protection are built up to shield against pain and potential hurt, you'll see an even less perfect circle.

The deeper the cut, the greater the need for the child to protect and defend itself. Every new hurt adds a new layer of protection, keeping others away from our core, away from where we're vulnerable and can be hurt — again.

The above sketch illustrates, on a physical level, how the protection makes us *bigger*. The perfect circle has become quite an unwieldy and much more sizable object. While every bump is built up to protect the sensitive parts, it also makes it more prominent, and because of the increased size more likely to run into obstacles and become aggravated all over again. The wound is now projecting to the surface like an antenna, and becomes more vulnerable, even though it lies deep beneath layers of protection.

Frustratingly, the very mechanism we developed for our protection now makes us more vulnerable, and a vicious circle begins as we add more layers, leading to a higher level of vulnerability by increasing the target area. We could call that self-defeating, and do so — when we recognize it in others.

While we don't have to accept this psychodynamic explanation, it nonetheless helps us understand what occurs on the emotional level. We're protecting ourselves through defence mechanisms which also make us increasingly more sensitive with each protective layer that contains its own vulnerability, since it reminds us of the hurt it is protecting and we start to perceive innocent comments as slights, and innocuous throw-away lines as directed to hurt us.

Me and my defences

What does this mean for relationships?

*A **very sobering conclusion: you never know a person, you only know their defences.***

It's a person's defences you use as a basis for liking or resenting them, to which you react and pass judgment. Taking it a step further, you only know a person through their defence mechanisms. Such defences include positively perceived behaviours, such as being 'nice', which may hide our tendency to lose it too quickly because of our high sensitivity. The same, of course, applies to any person who meets you. Only you know yourself — and even that only imperfectly.

As much as we recognize ourselves in the person we're attracted to, at the same time we're looking for someone to heal our wounds, give us what we were denied, craved, but only saw somewhere in the far distance. We want the one who makes our dreams come true, who complements us.

We also project our fantasies onto that person and infuse them in our own mind with the desire to meet our expectations. Meeting our needs means they're satisfying theirs as well, since they also want to be complemented. Pleasing us means they're also pleasing themselves, if only in our mind. The ideal complement.

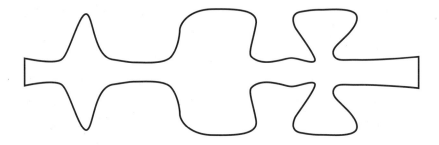

While it lasts, they are our 'perfect partner', our 'knight in shining armour', 'perfect princess' or our 'better half'. (Why *better*?)

But then the following occurs: Prince Perfect has the same need, at the same time, as Partner Princess. Compliments are a no-show now, expectations end in disappointment and the pieces don't fit so perfectly anymore. But we stay in the relationship, because we recognize we've found what we were looking for; it's just not available when we need it. This, in turn, can increase the feeling of frustration: 'I know you've got it! Why don't you show it to me or give me what I need? You miserable . . .'

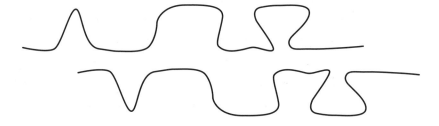

Now we're into the not-so-mysterious mechanisms of fatally attractive relationships. As you can see, there is nothing *fatal* about it, other than the violation of boundaries.

Accepting responsibility

If we stick to the principle of boundaries, we can recognize there's nothing wrong with the relationship or the partner. It's the *expectation* that does the damage, because it remains unexpressed, implied and most importantly, often subconscious.

To escape this trap you don't need to get out of the relationship; in fact, you'll likely end up in a new one desperately similar to the one you just ran away from. The answer lies in maintaining boundaries: you're responsible for your happiness and I'm responsible for mine. It's as simple as that. The difficulty can be in getting this message across without doing more damage to a fragile peace that may have just settled in.

This reality is therefore often better explained by someone outside the relationship. When I try to explain this mechanism and the conclusion in a counselling situation, I always suggest seeing both partners, to explain that this isn't a matter of their partner's egocentricity, but instead just a step towards repairing the relationship.

While dreams and expectations may provide the spark for a relationship, it has a better chance of surviving and thriving when each partner accepts responsibility for their own emotions and expectations — ultimately their own happiness.

A good start is to re-establish the content of the overlap in the circles on page 144, to give both partners the opportunity to be themselves and express themselves without feeling guilty. There is nothing wrong with establishing who I am, as opposed to who you are, including the rights and obligations that come with it. These are then newly defined as part of the binding relationship.

During that process, or because of it, the partners may realize there is nothing left between them that adds meaning to what they called a 'relationship'. It may lead to the dissolution of the partnership (personal, business or otherwise) but at least now they can go about it in a reasonable rather than emotional manner. You can agree to disagree without, or at least by limiting, hurt or disappointment.

Issues in relationships — intimate or otherwise

The law of attraction covered earlier also accounts for the fact that the longer, better or more intimately we know an individual the more likely it is they know how to hurt us or, as we would have put it previously, *know what makes us hurt*. They know what to say and do that hurts the most. And they do it on purpose (at least that's the assumption). We feel we have a right to be hurt and lash out, if not literally, then emotionally. Call it tit-for-tat, but it's understandable isn't it? Understandable it may be. Desirable? Definitely not. Necessary? Not at all. The answer again, is provided by the concept of boundaries and a boundary focus.

Since nobody can make you angry or frustrated it's futile to hold someone else responsible for your feelings. (I told you, think carefully before agreeing nothing and nobody can *make* you . . .) Why do we do it then? Could it be the habit we've formed over the years? Or is it easier to blame someone else instead of confronting the question about why we hurt, and what it means for you when your loved one says or does what they do and you *hurt*?

Often we find ourselves throwing tantrums, yelling, screaming and behaving in a very infantile manner indeed, as we would have to admit if we were honest with ourselves. This is even more difficult to accept when we're told so. So, how do we so frequently get away with behaving and reacting like a child?

The answer is because almost everyone does it at some time or another, and we're definitely all at risk in emotionally challenging situations of descending the developmental ladder. While generally rational beings, this seems only correct until our vulnerabilities are exposed, uncomfortably touched upon or threatened. At that point we start reacting in ways that others may call immature, driven not by reason but by emotion.

When we're feeling an emotion, remember to think of *energy*. Intent on building up energy for the purpose of defence, we then get rid of it again, like a steam engine builds up pressure not for the purpose of building up steam, but to drive the machine. Producing steam is only a means to an end — and so is the emotion we experience.

It's not an enjoyable state, because it's associated with danger. While we need to *get ready* we also want the danger to end so we can relax again. Screaming, punching a wall (or another person), slamming a door, turning up the radio so the neighbours have their bit of fun too, uttering expletives — all that helps get rid of this excess adrenaline. Were it not for the damage inflicted on some item, person or relationship, it would work perfectly. So, it's not the mechanism that is wrong — call it anger, frustration or snowpeas for all I care — it's the environment that makes our reaction inappropriate.

This could be the reason I haven't met anyone living by themselves who is deeply distressed by their own outbursts of anger. That's not to say that people living by themselves don't experience frustration.

They just do what they feel like doing, which isn't a problem, since nobody complains about it or gets hurt.

Conflict comes from at least two individuals having an emotional experience, which, however, can be shared in name only. The event is the same, but the emotions it raises are not, and never will be. At best I can second-guess what you might feel, since it all depends on your previous experiences in life, what they meant for you and what emotions they caused as a result. That determines what you say, how you react and what you expect of others.

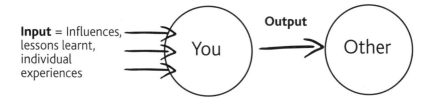

And this is what we're getting back:

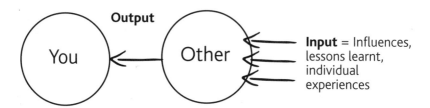

Because the nature of the arrows on the right are not the same as the ones on the left, we either argue until one gets blue (don't get picky on the colour, it could be purple) in the face, or we *respect* the experiences the other person brings to what usually starts as a conversation, before it descends into an argument or fight. Which of these possibilities prevails depends on the degree of respect we afford each other.

Here is a quick review of the reasons why we have such strong reactions, particularly towards the ones we love the most. As we've already seen, the first experience of feeling hurt occurs in early childhood, when the child is only able to process and accept it with a child's mind. The protection mechanisms it develops are based on the unsophisticated infantile level of processing of which it's mentally capable. The individual then carries these experiences, as well as the infantile defences, into adulthood and keeps reacting to any hurt in the same way it did when it was that defenceless child, with limited options for how to respond.

When we meet another person it takes time and familiarity before we let our guard down and make ourselves vulnerable to the same hurts we experienced way back when, even though we're now adults. Apart, of course, from our emotional brain, which is just so immature. It's the reason I call it our 'kid's brain'. It was never designed to grow up and think.

When our loved one speaks, we listen — for potential threats. The more protected our upbringing, the less we need to be alert. The more a child had to worry about the state of its closest relationships (it's also known as attachment), the one with its caregivers, the more vulnerable it is, and more likely in later life to perceive a threat, where in reality there may be none.

Any comment, vaguely perceived as criticism, has the potential to cross the threshold and trigger an alarm response, which then tends to create its own momentum, leading to accusations, and counter-defences, which results in increasingly convoluted relationships.

Boundaries to the rescue. Understanding the underlying reasons for these battles allows you in the first instance to reject a particular problem as being yours, even if you're told so all the time. Like an unwanted gift, you can hand the problem back; thanks, but no thanks.

Boundaries also make it possible to draw a line around particular issues, thereby preventing them from being brought up at every opportunity and meaning that you don't have to deal with the same issues again and again. By using boundaries, you can stop going round in circles.

The makings of interpersonal conflict

This is probably the most contentious area where we can apply the boundary approach. Of course, it's also the area where the model is likely to be the most helpful.

Imagine a movie where the plot line has no climax, no dramatic nexus, no social dilemma or otherwise. It would hardly be worthy of Oscar nomination; in fact, you'd probably call it boring.

What makes a movie exciting is when it becomes complicated. When diverging interests collide and the opportunities carry risks, when it asks for choices to be made between one value and another. And so it is in life. The more complicated it is, the higher our involvement and the more emotional energy we generate. With that come vested interests. When we give advice, we want and even expect it to be accepted and followed. But what if we couldn't care less? It wouldn't be a problem then, would it?

Falling in love really means someone else becomes important to us. We care about what they go through; it can almost feel as if what happens to them happens to us. What they lose hurts us just as much, if not more, because we not only feel sorry for their loss, we also feel sorry for how they feel — a double whammy. We worry about what they worry about, and we also worry about them.

The person we love is, of course, the person we *want to love*. They are the product of our introjections and projection of our own need for fulfilment. The projection of what we consider we need to be happy. 'I'll make you so happy for the rest of your life' can only mean my own version of what I *think* you want. Since I can't know what you really want at a given point in time, I introject my own feelings into you, assuming that's what you desire and therefore, what I think makes you happy. As a consequence, when I've done something for you, my expectation is that you're as content as I am now that I've done this great thing (whatever it may be) for you — in my own mind anyway. Like the very first example in this book of James and his contentious bunch of flowers. Hopefully now you can see why it didn't work out quite the way he intended.

You can see now, can't you, how important you are for me? Your reaction is absolutely vital to me, since it's the reason I've done what I did — which meets my needs as much as, I presume, it meets yours.

This is one of the reasons why the one you love has such great influence over how you feel. The greater the emotional investment the more you stand to lose. The similarity to financial investments is intended and appropriate, since they both involve risk, as far as that little *old* brain is concerned. It's not sophisticated enough to consider the quality, subject or nature of the investment. These considerations occur at a much later stage when all the information is being re-evaluated in the cerebral cortex. Obviously, the more we stand to gain, or lose, the higher our emotional sensitivity, the degree to which we're vulnerable and likely to feel slighted, hurt, attacked or that our needs are being ignored.

This situation of uncertainty about our partner's commitment and feelings towards us often precedes the arguments, misunderstandings and later silent acceptance or noisy separation of partners who were once madly, truly, deeply in love. How can that be avoided?

Obviously there can't be one answer to fit all situations and I do not propose to have the answer, but possibly I can offer a good starting point. Above everything else, the communication channels have to always stay open.

When disappointment strikes, the threat we may have always been so afraid of seems to materialize, friction is in the air and it becomes increasingly difficult to talk to each other in a rational fashion. With too much to lose, we play it safe: attack, and try to get an answer, but at the same time, not reveal too much in order to protect ourselves and not increase our vulnerability. The conversation — if it can be called that — becomes loud, acerbic and aggressive, or muted, sparse and we become reticent.

The result: a stalemate. Or it could be called a 'domestic argument' even though little may be spoken, as frosty silence prevails. The result is too often frustration rather than resolution, because the more we argue our point the more vulnerable we become. 'If I lose this one, I'm a goner,' says the amygdala deep within the brain, not being able to distinguish between friend and foe. When under attack, it doesn't make a difference that it may in fact be friendly fire. We may feel we're fighting a losing battle, because even winning is a loss at that point. But how can we stop what's happening?

The trick is to avoid this situation in the first place. 'Well, thanks for stating the obvious,' I hear you say, 'the question is *how*?'

Is this my problem?

Instead of considering the answer just yet, you may wonder what this has to do with boundaries.

Many words express the concept of boundaries: *limit, issue, extent* all equally describe this idea. Boundaries are the conceptualisation of separating, and seeing yourself as different from everybody and everything else. While self-evident it's just as easily forgotten. Before we know it we're roped in, agree to something without much consideration and eventually wonder how we ended up holding the baby when we weren't even pregnant.

Reminding yourself of this fundamental principle, that boundaries are what separate one thing from another, can give you more scope with regards to requests made of you, as well as sorting out what is not your problem, and what is — because you so choose.

I was approached by a young man once who asked if I could give him a lift in my car to the city, quite a distance away. He then told me he was only visiting and was now on his way back home somewhere overseas. Unfortunately, all his money, passport, traveller cheques, everything, had been stolen from his locker while he was working at a restaurant earning some travel money. I asked how he was going to get back home, or even to the airport, which was more than 100 kilometres away, and he told me he had no idea.

At this point, what would you have done? Taken him to the airport? Offered him money? How much? Only enough to get to the airport, or enough to buy himself a ticket back home? Would you have felt obliged to do anything?

We're likely to be struck by a sense of obligation to do something or work out what to say, if we're asked for help or money. (As it was the young man never asked for anything and it was left up to me if I wanted to do anything. I dropped him off somewhere where cars could easily pull in and stop and he could hitch another ride to the airport.)

It brought home, though, the first question for any such situation: 'Is this my problem?' If the answer is *yes*, deal with it; if it's *no*, make sure you really *want* to get involved before you do. In my case I had neither the money nor the time to help the young man any further.

As we've seen earlier, internalizing an issue means you'll now have a problem over which you have no control, because someone else owns it. You *chose* to become involved.

I therefore go as far as suggesting that when someone starts talking to you, you ask yourself: 'Is this my problem? Do I really want to answer?' before you even give an answer. Giving an answer can be the first step to a commitment you may have never wanted to make.

You may think this is taking it a little too far, but consider the following scenario. You work in an office and every morning the person at the front desk bids a friendly 'Good morning. How are you?' Without thinking you return the greeting and, being friendly, you add 'Fine. How are you?' The reality is you don't particularly like the person. Nonetheless, you're a friendly person and continue to return the greeting every morning. One day you happen upon that individual in the office kitchen. She starts a conversation. Since you've always returned her greeting by asking how she was, she believes you're interested in her wellbeing and starts to tell you her problems — personal, financial or otherwise, ultimately asking your advice: 'What shall I do?'

The fact is, you not only have no idea what to suggest, but you don't even care, nor do you want to hear all this. Too much information! But at what point do you make it clear you're not interested? My educated guess is, you won't. You either can't bring yourself to say it or there seems to be no right time to withdraw from the conversation. You'd probably feel guilty if you did.

Asking yourself 'Is this my problem?' first up would have allowed you to return the daily greeting with a friendly, simple *Good morning.* No '*How are you?*' No '*How are things?*' If you're not really interested one way or another, why invite a conversation you don't really want to have?

I'm very serious about the suggestion that you decide carefully about what you want to accept as your problem, and that it starts on the first level of engagement. Even then, and being discerning about what you say and do, you'll find yourself often enough in situations wondering, *how did I end up here,* or in situations you don't recall having invited into your life, which might overwhelm you.

To make '*Is this my problem?*' the first question to ask yourself when called upon or approached by someone may sound harsh and disengaged. However, it stems from listening to people telling me how they became caught up in a web of complex relationships from which they were unable to extract themselves. They seemed to have an inability to avoid becoming involved in such situations, and would only realize it when it all became too much. As for their future, it doesn't look any brighter. As soon as one situation is resolved, another one is bound to be waiting to engulf them.

Obviously, if you don't mind and have time and emotional capacity to burn, you don't need to worry about taking on someone else's problem. It may be the only one you have. Lucky you.

The practical benefits

For the rest of us it may be helpful to ask ourselves 'Whose problem is it anyway?' before it becomes too complicated. Getting used to answering this question for yourself helps you to develop emotional distance and be better prepared, especially in emotionally challenging situations.

Why is this useful? When we become emotional the right brain takes over and guides our actions. Since the faculty of speech is located on the left (and rational) side of the brain, the area where we experience emotions has no voice to articulate these experiences. The rational brain now tries to make sense of the signals it gets from the emotional brain, in other words out of something that makes no 'sense' since emotions are irrational. As we've seen earlier, words are only symbols for what we experience emotionally and can never convey what we uniquely feel as an individual.

Two people engaged in an emotionally charged conversation might as well speak different languages — and in fact they do. The more feelings are evoked as the conversation progresses, the further the two languages move apart and the only winner is frustration. And both will experience plenty of it.

Take an argument with your loved one. You may be reluctant to say what you think, because it could upset them. Well, whose problem is it then? By asking yourself that question you bring a 'third person' perspective into the conversation, which also introduces some emotional distance — and thereby some degree of rationality. Any conclusion based on emotions will only be a 'solution' until the next emotional challenge comes along, and throws everything into doubt again.

Any solution has to be based on reason-driven considerations, if it's to resolve the situation rather than only smooth it over.

If the other person 'chooses' (I don't really like that word, but you know what I mean) to get upset, angry, hurt or whatever else they may express, it's really not your problem. Why not? Because you don't know what effect your actions or words may have. You can only surmise and you may be right, or you could be wrong.

While your expectation may be based on experience, and your 'knowing' how they react (or vice versa; they *know* how you react, and say or do it anyway. Naughty!) on the downside it doesn't allow for changes that may have occurred and insights the person may have taken on over time. By pre-empting their response you push them into a corner and lock them into their old behaviour patterns, not allowing them the opportunity to change, or allow for the possibility they may have changed.

Assuming responsibility only for yourself and what you say and do, rather than the effects this may or may not have on someone else, allows for a new response pattern to emerge, which may be more constructive than the old one.

Anyone feeling uneasy or hurt by what you've done or said is at liberty to say so. Then you can respond to that situation, you can clarify it wasn't your intention and you were simply saying what was important to you. They can accept or reject that. Again, if they do or don't accept this it's not your problem and quite out of your control!

How someone's response to your words or action affects you, *that* is your problem, and you have to take responsibility for how you'll handle it and respond. In other words, *Is this my problem?* works in both directions. Drawing boundaries around what is and what isn't your problem allows you to change what you can control, rather than wasting your energy on issues that ultimately you can't control, and saves you all that frustration.

These boundaries allow each person to focus on what they can contribute to change the situation. While they may not like where they find themselves, they now know what they have to deal with and, more importantly, what is in and what is beyond their control. This simple fact, often only felt subconsciously, makes the situation more tolerable because it *contains* the situation.

As much as boundaries constrain, they also put limits around unpredictable and uncontrollable situations. That makes them reliable and, as you now know, this fact alone helps reduce any feeling of unease or stress. More importantly, though, it will lead you to real outcomes, not emotional conundrums you then have to try to unravel.

By asking yourself *Is this my problem?* first up, you allow yourself time to think before reacting. You can use the time to quickly assess if the situation you're confronted with has indeed been caused by you, your behaviour, what you said or did, or in fact has anything to do with you at all.

If the answer is yes, then the question — which of course, we prefer to perceive as an accusation, which makes it easier to counterattack — is just that, a question, and deserves an explanation or answer.

On the other hand, if the question involves an accusation you can't possibly disprove and you can only repeat whatever you may already have said before, then the problem isn't yours. It sounds instead as if someone has a problem believing what you say, and that is by definition *their* problem . . . which *you* can't solve.

In that case no matter what you say or do, the outcome is independent of your efforts. It will all depend on the other person, if they choose to accept what you have already said and how they decide to interpret it. All too often that may depend on their whim. Unless you like to subject yourself to someone else's whim, I suggest you don't accept it as your problem in the first place. Let them carry on if they must, but detach yourself: 'This isn't my problem, this is for you to work out. I can't do more than what I have done. If you can't believe me, I accept and respect that, and I also accept I can't do anything about it. I don't like it, but hey, such is life.'

I should add that it helps if the premise that nobody can *make* you do or feel anything if you don't want to has been discussed at a time when the mutual communication channels were still open. Preferably before you enter into any longer term commitment, such as marriage, civil union or partnership.

As I said before, and repeat it now for effect: start on a solid footing, and mutually agree that you can only *enhance* each other's state of contentment, but can't create it! If you should indeed have that power, it has been bestowed on you by the other person — and can just as easily be taken away again.

If this simple truth is put across with sufficient detachment, with an air that conveys the message 'I have to accept your decision on that, but I'm not buying into it because it's not my problem', it may open the door to improved communication. It could, of course, also lead to separation. Then again, it may have been headed in that direction anyway. Some things are inevitable.

Boundaries for couples in crisis

Working with couples, I've found a boundary focus very effective in containing the issues that have accumulated over time. Often many instances of discontent are brought into the counselling room in one big bundle, rolled up in great distress and with high or low expectations about the state of the situation. Previous efforts have helped to fortify emotions and attitudes and the therapist often gets only the latest version of the state of deadlock.

Relying on the story they've told me, I demonstrate where their expectations have clashed with (dis-)respect for the other person's opinion and right to make their own decision. They don't have to agree with that decision — in fact, they may strongly object. Or they may find they can't live with their partner's decision or action, in which case *that* is the issue to be resolved. Naming and isolating it gives them something to work on as a starting point for their disrupted communication, if they really want to resolve their differences. It's vital the conversation doesn't digress and other issues are introduced, even if they seem to be related. Any extension of the discussion runs the risk of also complicating issues again.

The inability to stick with one issue at a time indicates the need to win is still running the show and communication will suffer. Why? The will to win is an emotional need, and emotions have their own language, sometimes understood by lovers in their relationship, but not if it has turned into a *battle*ship.

Within the two circles I used earlier, the overlap is the focus and needs to be redefined. How this area affects each partner is a matter for them to resolve individually. Once they have come to a decision that reflects their non-negotiable needs, these can be acknowledged and the consequences for the partner — and themselves — can then be discussed.

This sets the direction for more fruitful conversations, and the basis for issues that have developed over time and need to be discussed within the framework of boundaries. *Let's just stick to this issue* replaces the rehashing of unfruitful arguments, which have been reiterated many times before.

When I introduce the concept of boundaries to couples in crisis, their feedback suggests they find the idea of being able to isolate issues and contain the sense of hopelessness that came with the problems they were facing comforting. Their deep sense of despair often stems from their belief that the issues are manifold, confusingly interwoven and overwhelming — and they're convinced there is no solution.

When they can see that each issue can be discussed individually, without the pressure of having to take responsibility for how their partner feels, it can have a liberating effect and a sense of hope returns. They may realize *I matter* and *I can say what I think* without being held responsible for how the other feels, and this may help to shift long-established and unhelpful mechanisms.

This may be an experience they haven't enjoyed for a long time, because of a well-intentioned but misplaced sense of responsibility for their partner's feelings. Being free of that perceived obligation also means being able to make decisions (*I don't want to talk about this now,* for example), and the formula *Unpredictability and no control = stress* can work its magic. Making a decision involves exercising control which results in the level of stress being lowered. In highly charged circumstances, even a small reduction in stress can be an enormous relief.

Introducing the concept of boundaries can also be helpful because it allows both partners to move away from external issues, back to themselves and their relationship. They can take a private moment to reflect and decide for themselves if there's enough love left for the relationship to continue. They can decide before they turn back to each other if *I love you* is still backed up by a feeling or if *love* has returned to simply being a four-letter word. If there is enough feeling, they can renegotiate the shared space that defines their relationship, their intimacy.

I can't deny a boundary focus can also present a great challenge for a partner, particularly when one is hurting while the other has already moved on. Being in pain, being emotional, means their ability to accept a rational approach is compromised. Such an approach might then be perceived as heartless and be unwelcome. Why do I suggest it nonetheless? Because ultimately they'll have to face the reality that everybody can only be responsible for themselves and their own feelings. Only they can deal with the hurt and pain they are experiencing. More importantly, heartless as the fact is, we *can't* make anybody feel what they don't feel anymore.

Just to make sure, this is only the beginning of what needs to happen in subsequent conversations or counselling sessions. But it can be a powerful opener to more specific work on individual issues. Just as looking at a signpost doesn't get you where you want to go — it just tells you where you have to go, and if you make the effort, you can get there.

11. **Boundaries in other relationships**

When I apply a boundary focus to specific situations, I rely on the following premises. Problems result from overlapping boundaries. When boundaries are crossed the outcome is unpredictable in a similar way as when chemicals are mixed, depending on their quality and what they are blended with. Recognition of — and respect for — boundaries allows you to remedy their violation and thereby recreate a degree of predictability, which is one of the basic human needs.

This by itself won't necessarily resolve all conflicts, but it can often be a useful first step towards resolution by drawing a line around issues and thereby providing a starting point for constructive discussions. It can also help each individual draw a boundary around their own feelings, and help them to stay with one issue at a time and not become overwhelmed by a number of often conflicting feelings.

For parents

When it comes to the relationship between a parent and a child, a boundary focus has to take account of the fact that in the early stages of development the two circles used earlier almost overlap.

However, from a very early age children want to know boundaries exist. It's their aim when they venture out and start to explore their environment. They want to be able to orient themselves, which is only possible within a set of boundaries, be they physical, or exist as rules. It gives them the assurance of knowing where they are in relation to their next point of safety, and ultimately in relation to their total environment. As adults we can greatly assist children, even when they're not our own, to learn about boundaries, what is allowed and what not, where you can and can't venture, and so on.

The difficulty parents often experience as their child gets older is when to increase the child's slice of the circle and acknowledge their growing independence. For young children boundaries are dictated by a parent's obligations to safety and care. As they get older this changes and now your respect for their boundaries increasingly has to take precedence. It starts in adolescence and culminates when they have their own families and live independent lives.

It's often tempting to be soft when reinforcing boundaries for one's child, because it seems easier to give in, with fewer tantrums and often a lower noise level to contend with. The thought may creep into your head that a child is a 'free spirit' and knows better than you what's good for them and what they need. After all, these are cultural restraints you're trying to enforce and you might find yourself thinking *my child can grow up free and make up their own mind in time.*

Once you've finished with those thoughts, you're welcome to join the real world again.

Children may not like the content or extent of boundaries, but need and continuously search for them.

Just as it is for adults, although we may be loathe to admit it, it's comforting to know that boundaries exist. While they restrict our freedom, they also represent predictability and reduce our stress level.

As the child becomes older, it's not only mandatory to set up and reinforce boundaries, it's equally important to *maintain* boundaries when discussing different issues, particularly with older children or teenagers. Very often a question turns into an argument because we bring in, or allow them to introduce, issues that have little to do with the question being discussed. Isolating the issue and identifying exactly the question or problem makes it a lot easier to find an answer. This teaches young children to stay with one issue, and becomes increasingly important as they grow up, helping to make their world less convoluted. Remember, adolescence is a time of growth but also a time of great confusion. Simplifying a situation helps you as much as it gives them some relief.

Don't expect instant gratitude, though. Overt signs of appreciation may take a little longer to eventuate. Even if it never occurs, feel reassured that children love boundaries; in fact, they thrive on them. Proper boundaries and proper boundary setting is the difference between the concept working or failing. Inconsistent boundary setting is as bad as having no boundaries. It leaves them with no concept of their own position in the world.

*What goes for setting boundaries also goes
for maintaining them. Your obligation to set
boundaries extends to your obligation to also
respect your children's boundaries, rights,
privacy, decision-making — whatever you care
to call it.*

Sure, it's hard to watch your child making what you see as a mistake.
But for them it's only their life the way they want to live it, no matter if
you like it or not. There is always your duty to prevent physical harm,
particularly for younger children, but be careful not to extend this
obligation, particularly if you're serving your own interest more than
your child's.

Hard to swallow? Yes, but also a reasonable premise, since
they could likewise expect you to live *your* life according to *their*
expectations — for example, *downsize your home and give me the
extra cash* — a proposition which is just as reasonable as you offering
unsolicited advice to your grown-up child. If you do offer advice at
this stage, don't expect it to be followed.

Awareness of the existence of boundaries is particularly helpful
in so-called blended families. It allows you to clarify in your own
mind, as much as with your partner, which boundaries are and are
not negotiable. You can set out from the start very clearly what *your*
kids and *my* kids means. Are you allowed to tell them what to do, and
set the limits?

This helps not only to clarify boundaries, it also brings out
differences in opinion early in the relationship, which is preferable to
waiting until boundaries have been crossed and unhelpful response
patterns established.

Friendships

I pointed out earlier that you may conclude it's safest to draw a very wide boundary around yourself and generally stay away from people, because with every step you take towards someone you increase the risk of misunderstandings and boundary violations. Correct!

Does that mean we should stay away from people and close relationships? Of course not! Again, it's not a problem if it's not a problem.

The boundary-focused approach has two aims: to make you aware of what's occurring when two people meet and enter into any kind of relationship; and to provide a direction when a relationship no longer meets mutual needs.

Boundary violations occur often not through deliberate actions, but as the result of innocent enough assumptions and sometimes an overly casual approach to others and their rights and needs. You could call it a lack of respect for who they are and what they are entitled to, or 'taking them for granted'.

While awareness allows you to tread more carefully from the start, helping you become more considerate for lack of a better word, it does *not* protect you from difficulties in a relationship.

In relationships based on friendship the difficulty can often be the unspoken assumptions we make. As with intimate relationships, the content of boundaries isn't always clear. But while in intimate relationships we've more contact and more opportunities to clear up any misunderstandings, we generally don't have as much opportunity in friendships, since we only usually meet to enjoy a good time in each other's company.

Disagreements are much rarer in friendships than in intimate relationships, which can lead to the assumption they don't exist. That makes it then so much more painful when they do show up. Instead of treating a disagreement as an individual event we tend to generalize and then question the nature and quality of the friendship, sometimes coming to the conclusion that 'We weren't friends after all'.

Resist that urge. It's a dramatization, an irrational response to the emotional reaction we call *disappointment*. Treat it rationally and you might discover your friend only expressed their individuality. With this perspective you'll continue to enjoy exactly what you appreciated in them before.

Remind yourself in such situations that you (!) overstepped the boundary with your particular expectation. There's no need to hold your friend responsible for your feelings and the fact they didn't react or behave in the way you wanted. It's their right, even if, or rather *because*, you are friends!

In these cases setting and maintaining boundaries can give your relationship more substance. If you establish who you are, what you can and can't rely on, what your needs are and, most of all, *each assumes full responsibility for their own happiness*, you both have a reasonable basis (i.e. based on reason, not emotions) for the future of your relationship. This may well mean you decide to go your separate ways, but it will also mean you can do that while still, if not remaining friends, at least being civil.

12. **Boundaries applied 'clinically'**

A boundary-focused approach can also be applied to 'clinical' issues. Such an approach accepts that every issue, situation, individual or relationship is essentially an independent entity, external to every other one. This focus presents the opportunity for a slightly different take on what is generally considered a disorder, and then also suggests a different treatment approach.

As individuals we choose to make connections or create relationships between these individual units, be they persons, relationships, ideas or issues. Making these connections is based on our personal experiences, convictions and expectations and the way we connect them is as much the cause for discomfort as it is unavoidable. By making these links we necessarily cross, or at the very least blur, boundaries. Staying aware of them allows us to step back, reassess the situation and revisit and revise decisions we made or are about to make.

Decision is the operative word here, since every time we make a decision it means we're exercising control — and we make a previously unpredictable situation a little less so. This process increases our sense of subjective wellbeing (aka SWB), because it reduces the level of threat the brain perceives and reacts to. The concept of boundaries can help achieve just that, so let's see how this can now be applied to areas such as depression, anxiety and social anxiety.

Depression

Let me first state that depression can be a serious illness. It's not to be taken lightly and professional advice should always be sought. There are different kinds of depression, though, that differ significantly in the way they can be treated. The following is appropriate for times when you feel down but are still able to make decisions. We might also experience this feeling when things seem to pile up, and we feel somewhat dejected because a solution to our problems seems a long way off.

When, and if at all, depression needs to be diagnosed as an illness is difficult to determine, since all illnesses are defined by the way their symptoms result in a deviation from the parameters of normal. What is normal, however, is determined by what most people do, which by itself is neither desirable nor undesirable, but depends on how we view 'the norm'.

That most young people spend time on their mobile phones or computers, for example, can be seen as quite undesirable, because of the ill effects we experience now or expect in the future. But because this behaviour can be viewed as something *they all do* it could be defined as normal. Despite being quite annoying or even interfering in normal human interaction, it's not currently defined as maladaptive.

Likewise, what we now call depressed may at a different time have been experienced as normal. To qualify as a poet in the 19th century these feelings may even have been an essential part of the job description. Yet in the 20th century and with the arrival of television shows (which projected happy endings and the sense that *normal* families resolve all problems) the idea of happiness shifted. This sense of not being what television and other media suggested as desirable was often interpreted as unhappiness, with the next step being depression.

The development and increasing use of psychoactive drugs (read pharmaceutical companies) willingly supported the widening of the diagnostic criteria. What was previously experienced as normal was increasingly diagnosed as an illness, since such unpleasant mood states could now supposedly be chemically treated. While on a subjective scale individuals may not have felt any different years earlier, they now experienced their feelings as much more unpleasant.

That is not to say that there are no cases of severe depression. The question is only whether these could have been prevented through earlier interventions.

Signs of depression are like any warning lights alerting us to the need to take steps to address the causes. The more delay before the response, the worse the problem will become, otherwise there would be no reason for the warning signals. Do you keep driving your car if the light comes on telling you there's not enough oil in the engine or water in the radiator? You do so at your peril.

Boundaries and 'me'

The answer to the question *What's wrong with me?* is simple: nothing. Something *wrong* implies it has to be changed. For an individual, having something *wrong with me* means they have to change *who they are* to feel better. A boundary focus suggests a different approach.

Often, depression can be seen as a symptom of a seemingly overwhelming situation. Interventions with a boundary focus treat the symptoms of depression as a functional indicator of the brain and body responding to the clues they provide for each other. After all, they are both part of the same system. If your legs get tired, you sit down and rest them. What do you do when your mind gets tired?

Rather than having to change and become someone else, a boundary-focused approach emphasizes that you have choices when dealing with these challenges. You can draw a line around the individual issues that have piled up and appear as one single, enormous task; you can then decide what to do about each issue one at a time. You don't have to change yourself, but instead change the way you apply who you are to each circumstance.

Often this isn't easy — it may seem unpalatable, involve sacrifices or a high degree of re-adjusting because issues may be difficult to disentangle. However, this isn't the problem, but rather part of the solution. Having, or becoming aware of, alternatives and the availability of choices changes the situation from overwhelming to manageable. Instead of feeling at the bottom of the pile, you're sitting on top and able to sort out and throw away unwanted ballast.

I find it useful to think of depression as an ultimate feeling of being overwhelmed, burdened by the number of events that seem to happen 'all at once'. Each event by itself would normally be tolerable, but with their combined weight they seem unbearable. A focus on boundaries allows me to tease out each issue as a stand-alone item that can be resolved, one at a time, in order to start getting some relief. It's not necessary to attend to the whole pile of problems all at once.

The overwhelming problem is no longer *within* but *outside* of me. It's something I deal with rather than something I experience, and that puts distance between me and the problem. Rather than feeling things being forced upon me, I can now extend or reduce this distance, and it's a decision I alone make.

By treating an issue as *out there* rather than *in here*, it's given its proper place — something you choose to accept, but that doesn't *oppress you* . . . unless you let it.

Anxiety

Anxiety is the fear of something that may or may not occur. It's the right response in the wrong circumstances, or at the wrong time. There's nothing wrong with this response itself, except for the timing. Trying to get rid of anxiety is like trying to stop chewing before swallowing food. It's not a healthy thing to do.

Using that metaphor, there's no point chewing if there's nothing in your mouth. There's nothing wrong with chewing as an activity, except for looking a bit strange, and being a waste of energy if there's nothing to chew. This isn't altogether unlike how anxiety functions: why would you start to 'chew on' fear when in reality you haven't got anything to be afraid of or worry about?

Without the body being able to produce the feeling of fear we wouldn't have survived. Fear is necessary to alert us to danger. What we call fear today is no more than the body activating its energy resources to be able to — you guessed it — bash or dash.

Anxiety seems to confront us with the conundrum I mentioned earlier, that we consider ourselves as humans, and therefore as rational beings. However, anxiety is irrational and if it strikes, reason disappears at the same rate as our fear takes hold. Thousands of years of evolution that resulted in the development of our rational brain — gone! It seems another indication that we're more animal than we'd like to admit.

As much as emotions allow for the most intense experiences

of happiness, they also manage to get in the way and cause us the greatest despair, sometimes in short succession, and no more evident than when anxiety strikes. In the case of anxiety, not only does arousal enable us to react to threats and survive, it can also manage to get us into trouble — to the point of endangering our lives. Imagine defending yourself against a perceived attacker, who was in fact simply trying to return your lost wallet. When feeling threatened like this, you could rely on the statistical likelihood of something not happening and hope for the best. Conversely, if you defend yourself and the attack wasn't real, you're in trouble. If you don't do anything and the attack is real, you're in trouble.

This is pretty much the situation for people who suffer from anxiety. What seems real (danger) is often not, and what doesn't seem real to them (safety) they're told to trust as being real. Quite a big ask.

As is the case for depression, there's nothing wrong with the brain's response to a perceived threat. What you feel is normal, but for the timing. Fear of tigers is very useful if I were visiting India; it would prevent me from jumping out of the car to give the big pussycat a cuddle. However, in my usual suburban home environment this same fear would be somewhat misplaced. In this scenario what is supposed to ensure my survival now works against me.

The object of my anxiety doesn't have to be physically threatening; it might be fear of disease or a car accident. The crippling effects of anxiety mean that in the extreme you can't move outside your home, and even within it you have to draw the curtains to achieve a sense of safety.

When fear takes hold it tightens the chest like a vice, breathing becomes difficult, eye contact is almost impossible and the thought of having to meet social obligations becomes an ongoing torture often followed by feelings of worthlessness and ineptitude. It's small wonder that depression is a frequent companion of anxiety. How can we make sense of this and, more importantly, what can you do when anxiety strikes?

Since we see danger where there is none, anxiety is essentially and literally a waste of energy, because it's not needed. Anxiety is the result of the body releasing stress hormones to make energy available. The breathing changes from normal to quick, short gasps, which in effect increases the oxygen content in the blood. The more oxygen we have, the more energy is available. The quicker and shorter the breathing, the more the sufferer becomes aware of the thumping of their heart. The thought may occur that a heart attack might be nigh, since the symptoms we feel are now quite similar.

The result is hyperventilation, an anxiety or panic attack and ultimately the loss of consciousness. This process started as a perceived threat and ends up being a real threat.

What has happened, of course, is that the boundary between objective and subjective reality has been crossed. If we think within a boundaries paradigm, it's a matter of separating one from the other. I can indulge my fears as much as I can indulge my wishful fantasies. The problem is, we draw a clear boundary when we wish, and know it's not real, but we fail to do the same when we're feeling anxious.

A challenge to your thoughts: what's the evidence?

Knowing what you're dealing with is one thing; how to deal with, or better, how to prevent something negative from occurring, is another. So, what can you do?

In the first instance we need to acknowledge that anxiety doesn't occur in a vacuum. Preceding the attack is a build-up of energy, which eventually leads to the feeling of anxiety. If you experience the onset as striking *without warning*, it's usually associated with an identifiable event you failed to consciously register, that triggered the fear response. In order to bring about awareness of the trigger or to stop the escalation process, there are a number of strategies, which by themselves or in combination can help to prevent anxious feelings spiralling out of control.

First of all, if there is a reason for your fear, *do* something about it.

It's important to listen to your fears, but it's not always helpful to give in to them.

Becoming aware of the thoughts that lead to feelings of anxiety is helpful, but sometimes it also can be the problem, because the sufferer only pays mind to their anxiety when it's already too late. Awareness can then simply accelerate the unhelpful thoughts. Sufferers often describe the feeling of being *out of control* of their own thoughts. This is a frightening experience, and for good reason. For one, who wants to have their thoughts controlled by someone or something else? Secondly, as discussed, a lack of control contributes to stress. While it's scary if your thoughts feel out of your control, the question to ask here is, are they?

It can certainly feel that way. The worst experience seems to be the same thoughts recurring, or involving the same theme. But if you're not in control of your thoughts, exactly who is?

Now we're back in the land of reality. I have it on good authority, and supported by research, that there is no evidence of some little man (or woman) up there in the brain pushing buttons and pulling levers, controlling what you think. This leaves me to conclude it's *you* who has control over your thoughts. You may just have forgotten how to exercise it. As it is in every other situation where a vacuum appears, someone or something else will fill it if you don't. It's a simple observation of nature, and not only human nature.

Consider your brain as a very helpful but a little over-eager servant. When you're anxious it observes what you're thinking, and since you're following every thought it provides for you, it's only too eager to go through the whole hard drive and bring up whatever it can lay its feelers on most quickly. In other words, the more you follow your racing thoughts, the more your brain will throw up new ones, until it gets tired of looking for new material and simply repeats the repertoire.

Particular thoughts are linked to established thought patterns, which when activated evoke particular feelings, which usually accompany these thoughts. This forms the now detrimental sequence your brain follows. Hebb's Law of how neural networks are created states: what fires together, wires together. The thoughts activate the feelings, which further activate linked thoughts associated with the pattern you have established, activating associated neural networks, and so on. The result is 'looping thoughts'.

Remember your thoughts are simply 'neurons firing'. There is no external reality to their content. Nobody would know by simply looking at you what you're thinking. Nor does it make any difference to the outside world. If you don't control your thought processes it causes grief only in your own head and doesn't affect anything outside of yourself in a direct way. If you're not convinced of this, imagine winning the next state lottery and see what happens . . . have you won yet?

Thoughts can't hurt you, because they are only thoughts. Secondly, if you can produce the thoughts you can also stop them.

In fact, *only you* can stop this particular neural activity. Remember, there's no little man up there flicking switches making you think or worry, and also nothing and no one can make you feel or do anything. This concept works for your thoughts as much as for anything else. You make things happen all by yourself, including your thoughts.

So how do you take control over your thoughts, which, when you're consumed by anxiety, seem to fall over themselves to annoy you? Think of a computer that has several applications open, while you only use one at a time. That doesn't mean the other programs have disappeared. You may have minimized them or they're hidden behind the document you're working on, but they're still there, running in the background.

Something very similar happens with the thoughts in your mind: they're always there, whether you pay attention to them or not. If you can activate them and call them into your conscious thought, you can also *minimize* them and put them at the bottom of the screen — or the back of your mind.

Although you may not always be aware of it, the mind is active on several levels at any one time. For example, if your partner tells you in the morning not to forget the milk when you come home from work, you might remind yourself occasionally through the day but won't think about it all day long. You focus instead on your work, which may involve switching between different tasks.

Then you leave work and suddenly remember the milk. All the while that thought had been in the back of your mind, even though you were oblivious to it for most of the day. If it wasn't there all along, how could you have remembered it later? Remembering is retrieving something that has always been present. If we *really* forget, it's just as if we never knew the information and we wouldn't be able to remember it later and could deny any prior knowledge.

While this seems confusing it simply means a thought at any given time is only part of the brain's activity, it's only the activity we're aware of, not the full activity log. The proper way to describe what we conventionally call forgetting is probably a case of forgetting to remember at a particular time.

When you apply this to racing thoughts, the only difference to your normal thinking is that you're aware of and paying attention to the many things your mind is doing. Don't be angry with it. Just rein it in and let it relax. Focus on one thought, and allow the other thoughts to swirl around in the background, just don't pay any attention to them. They'll eventually go away because your brain has no interest in keeping something going you don't find important. Why would it?

If this sounds too simple to be true, consider that it happens every time you talk with someone. Although they may stand in front of a painting, a building or even among other people, you only pay attention to the conversation. In this scenario of course you're not unaware of the background, because if something interesting suddenly happened, you would switch your attention instantly.

At the same time you couldn't say you noticed it, because as the attention is on the conversation, we reduce or minimize everything in the background. This is a case of parallel processing, where we only focus on one thing at a time while subconsciously taking in a whole lot more information, which may later suddenly pop into our consciousness.

The difference between conscious and subconscious processing is *attention*. What we attend to is what we're aware of, but that doesn't mean our brain stops processing other incoming information. So, when controlling your thoughts let the mind do what it does, and simply choose your own focus, noticing the other thoughts that may drift in and out of your consciousness, but not paying mind to them.

A word of caution: never, ever tell yourself *I don't want to think about this* when you want to stop a thought. What you're really telling your brain is this: *When that thought occurs, forget it.* Logically, to be able to forget that thought the brain first has to remember which thought it's supposed to forget. That means it has to remember what you told it to forget. So without fail you'll keep thinking about it.

If you don't want to think about something, switch your attention, or tell yourself you don't want to think about it *now*, that you'll do so later and set yourself a particular time or occasion. Now your intention is subject to the same process of forgetting (or minimizing) as the milk you were supposed to bring home — and remember just as you turn into your driveway.

Breathing

There's a practical way to control your feelings of anxiety, however the catch is you have to use it as soon as you become aware of anxiety rising within you. If you leave it too late, you'll not only forget to do it, but also how to do it.

Hyperventilation messes up the delicate balance between O_2 and CO_2, which results in light-headedness, a tingly sensation in the extremities and a range of other disconcerting bodily activities and sensations, which all return to normal once balance is restored.

A technique that prevents a build-up of CO_2 is regular diaphragmatic breathing, breathing into the abdomen and exhaling slowly — see page 214 for a detailed explanation. When you first set out to control your feelings of anxiety, do it every hour on the hour or, every time you sit down at your desk; use any prompt that reminds you to 'take a deep breath'.

The regular slowing down of your breathing ensures not only that your blood chemistry is kept in balance, but also serves as a reminder to keep a check on your thoughts.

Social anxiety versus self-esteem

Feelings of anxiety are often experienced when around other people, and can occur even in otherwise well-adjusted individuals. The thought that others may be watching and judging us doesn't have to be debilitating, but can be quite uncomfortable and disconcerting. The thought of not being *good enough*, not keeping up in the looks department, having an inferior job or the like can make us feel as if we're being judged and that we're coming up short. But what's really happening here?

Feeling judged and inadequate is our individual experience despite the lack of hard evidence. We're again victims of our imagination of our own shortcomings. If we tend to judge others we're also likely to expect others to do the same, and judge us. Remember *Your opinion of another person* on page 109?

Instead of being afraid of what others think, work on your own tendency to judge others. That *is* under your control. What others may or may not think about you *is not*.

There's another aspect to our fear of being judged by others. It's based on a lack of self-esteem. We may feel unworthy and inadequate, and describe ourselves in less glorious terms than we would see others. Here's the conundrum: if you're so inadequate, why would anyone bother to take any notice of you, either to judge or otherwise make any reference to you? Not quite logical, is it?

Here are two possible answers.

Either you take yourself more seriously than you'd like to admit, or there's no need to feel embarrassed since nobody takes any notice of you anyway. Isn't that liberating!

From now on you have the freedom to do as you please because people either won't bother to pay attention, or you can decide that you won't give a damn if they do. If you do take yourself more seriously than you admit, my question is, do you really think you're that important and other people have nothing better to do than to focus on whatever you're doing, wearing or saying? You can answer that question for yourself, but whatever the outcome, do you still worry about people who have nothing better to do than focus on other people?

Stirred and shaken: thoughts mixed with emotions

Clients often complain about being bothered by *worry thoughts*. Again, this is a violation of boundaries, because we combine two different concepts.

One is a rational fact, a thought. The other is an emotional reaction, an emotional fact, if you wish. When we combine and treat them as one, it becomes a reason to worry, so to speak. By treating them as separate entities, a thought and an emotional reaction to it, we also have the key to protecting ourselves from the commanding nature of a *worry thought*.

I can think about anything in an abstract way, even my own death, and remain very rational and unemotional; for example, when signing up for a funeral plan or writing my last will — hoping it won't be my last. I may even joke about it. However, if a day later my doctor tells me that if I want to buy a book to read I'd better make it a short story, my detached way of treating my impending death would probably dissolve and I could easily imagine becoming quite emotional.

That's the difference between a thought and a 'worry thought' or 'a worry'. This fact allows us to think about anything we like without getting upset, if we can keep our emotional distance.

To help you do that, keep this difference in mind. If you want to think about an issue, contemplate it, but put the emotions that arise in their place. 'Not now' can be helpful in this respect. Allocate a time when you'll allow yourself to explore the emotional dimension of the thought, when you'll determine the impact.

Whatever you do, exercise control. Who's in charge here after all? Since it's you, assert your authority over your own thoughts!

Anger (and other emotions) management

When it comes to anger the expectation is that you can control your anger, and I've had clients come to me requesting help to do precisely this. At other times it's referred to as anger management. What's the difference, and does the terminology itself make a difference? Control and management are almost diametrically opposed concepts. When we try to control something, we reject it and want to subdue it. Managing something, however, implies that we allow it to exist and redirect or manipulate the way it's used or expressed. I apply the latter to emotions.

Unpleasant, so-called 'negative' emotions are the reaction to something that doesn't suit our plans. As such it's a potential threat and essentially we have two options, withdrawal accompanied by sadness and tears, or anger, expressed by some more or less violent act. Look closer and you'll realize we're dealing with two different issues. One is about the action we observe, the other the emotion we infer behind the action. The result is a circular argument as we saw when we talked about emotions in Part 1.

To appreciate how easily actions and the emotions behind them can be confused, take the example of someone smashing up a house. Are you watching someone who is angry, or someone who's at work? Just because a person is doing a demolition job does it mean they're not angry when they're doing it? They could well have had an argument with their boss, which they take out on the building they demolish. And if they do, does that turn their legal activity into an offence? Obviously, the circumstances determine if the destruction is illegal or part of a demolition job, not the emotion behind it.

We know different people interpret what they see differently. What some call tough, others may call cold-blooded. Empathy can be seen as weakness, anger or sadness. If we know a person more intimately, we may also assign different attributes to their actions, compared with someone we only just met.

You might also think of a crying child. Are they sad or frustrated? Have they hurt themselves or do they just want to be held? Are they angry, afraid or simply tired? Even if you knew more of the circumstances, you still couldn't be sure it's not a combination of all of these (frustration, for example, because they're tired and miss their mother). This illustrates how fallible emotional labels can be.

When we observe, or rather perceive, a particular emotion we use our own frame of reference to decide how someone feels or why they act the way they do. This then also guides our response; for example, we might perceive an argument while your partner calls it a conversation.

After all this, what exactly are we talking about when we speak about managing anger? Our reaction to something that happens around us (a sound, an event, or even the absence of something we expect to happen) is the subjective aspect of the emotion we feel. What we experience obviously isn't pleasant, or we would be happy and content. Our primitive brain processes it as a threat. Now the switch has been flicked and we experience an energy surge.

This energy is what we experience as anger (or in fact, any emotion). It drives our anger outburst, or what we would subsume under the 'fight' response. As a result we 'attack' something or get into a more or less physical confrontation with a person. The result is the same. The pent-up adrenaline is released through the physical activity of punching, swinging or shouting, and we feel better. However, this relief is short-lived and only lasts until we have to deal with the fall-out of our action and we despair at the silliness of what we've done, profess we didn't mean it and won't do it again.

We've previously discussed emotions as linked to the survival mechanism in the brain, and if left unchecked they'll override reason. When we react to some real or perceived threat, we still literally use the physical and developmental 'bottom' of our brain. Although we subsequently developed the capacity to think and calmly consider our options, using this capacity often seems optional. And all the while we think we're being 'reasonable' creatures in the first place.

In practice, the more emotional you get, the less reasonable you'll act.

Remember this diagram?

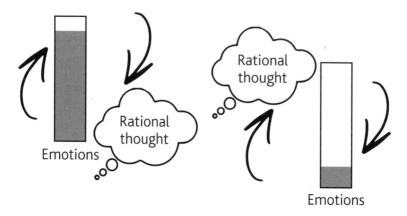

Think of it as the distribution of your energy. The more energy needed to fuel your emotions, the less you have left to spend on thinking rationally.

When you feel your survival is threatened, as far as the limbic system is concerned, everything else is insignificant.

When you think or feel you're under attack nothing else matters, because if you don't survive why worry about your last tax bill?

Because we're supposed to be rational beings, after the event we feel compelled to find an explanation, an excuse — or a 'reason' for our feeling, and our subsequent actions. In retrospect that often sounds contrived, and we tend to dismiss it as an attempt to make up excuses. However, for the individual involved it's only an attempt at trying to make sense out of something that's emotion-driven and therefore senseless.

This 'excuse' phase is particularly painful for all adversely affected by your anger outburst, who feel you're making excuses (which you do) and that nothing will change. Unless you find a more helpful explanation for your anger, which also allows you to find different ways of releasing that energy, they may well be correct.

Managing emotions

The clue for how to manage anger is buried in the explanation of emotions, namely as the release of energy. Rename anger as 'energy', and you also get an idea of what may work best for you to release this energy other than through ineffective actions.

Being told to 'control your anger' is about as helpful as suggesting to breathe when you're underwater. But let's say you were asked to manage your energy level, how would you go about it? Would you do it in one explosive outburst, or in a more measured way? By destroying or by creating something? Through letting off steam or thinking about solutions?

'Managing emotions' is simply another way of suggesting you

'manage your energy level' — except the latter is decidedly more helpful. On a physical level you could go for a run or engage in some other kind of physical activity. Digging up the garden may be more productive than smashing something to smithereens or having an argument. You can apply this to any of your feelings and you'll find an answer that suits you. Ask yourself how you can most productively get rid of energy, rather than the emotion you assigned to it.

Keeping your focus on what has been said or done (and has already annoyed you) only increases your energy level and makes an 'angry' reaction more likely, particularly if this has been your usual response pattern. Old learned behaviour patterns, such as what we think others may expect of us, are also likely to take over. Changing your thinking, and relabelling the feeling as a surge of energy may, for example, remind you not to let a fight get in the way of enjoying yourself.

When you address this 'energy' issue without prejudice, you may find there are more stressors in your life than you were previously aware of. They could be financial stressors, worries about job security, marital discord, including sexual frustration — any of these on their own or in combination could result in the release of excess adrenaline, which leaves you feeling angry. Talking to a therapist can help unlock these unconscious concerns and bring them to your awareness.

Considering we're talking about the energy that fuels the fight or flight response, anything is probably better than following your immediate instincts. Associating the feeling of anger with energy can help to distract from the reason for your energy surge. Since we try to find reasons for our feelings (the mind always tries to create predictability) we can soon come up with one; the kids are too loud, your partner's not doing what you wanted, the car's not fuelled up and so on.

If getting physical isn't an option, simply take some time out for a breathing exercise. Diaphragmatic breathing (see page 214) is by far the most effective short-term relief. I see anger as an oversupply of oxygen, and since oxygen equals energy (think of pumping yourself up before heavy lifting or athletes before the starting gun) the less oxygen, the less energy you have available. Although physiologically it's not quite that simple, it's a neat equation to remember when the adrenaline rush hits and your breathing changes into over-drive.

Chronic pain management

We sometimes hear pain is 'all in the head', so let me clarify that pain (perception) is indeed in the head (where else?), but originates in different parts of the body. Second, when talking about pain management, I refer here to chronic pain.

That pain is in the head is evidenced by the phenomenon of phantom pain. Even when a limb is amputated, the person can still feel pain —and I mean excruciating pain — and discomfort in that limb, as the neural connections of the amputated part still exist in the brain.

The concept of boundaries can be helpful in pain management through focusing on the sensation of pain, rather than trying to avoid it. Concentrating on the origin of the pain sensation, its location and intensity, you can draw an imaginary circle around the pain. Within that circle you can observe how it changes and how the sensation (rather than pain) varies at different times. Give pain a boundary and then contain it within that circle.

You can also develop a relationship with your pain, strange as it may sound, as with someone you know but might not necessarily like too much, though are friendly with. You can then have a conversation with your pain, take it out for a walk or a coffee, literally or in your mind, and keep it in its place. Rather than letting it become all encompassing, all consuming, you can contain the pain within its boundary, live and work with it, rather than suffer trying to fight against it.

Avoid internalizing your pain. Treat it as an external issue, not something you identify with that defines who you are.

The wish to be pain-free probably plays as big a part in the experience of pain as the nerve impulse itself, but also impedes our ability to 'live with it'. That requires a degree of acceptance, the acceptance that it won't go away, to be precise. On the other hand, accepting the pain sets you free to take the next step — making it manageable rather than submitting to it.

Chronic pain often dictates the life of the sufferer and they start to identify with the pain as if there's no existence without it. Yet, there are often days when the pain is less, sometimes even forgotten. As in most situations (except the most extreme cases), when our focus is occupied by other more interesting events, we 'forget' about the pain.

Consider the following. Let's say you burnt yourself severely because of someone's, even your own, carelessness. What feeling would accompany your pain? Anger? Frustration? Regret? Contrast that with approaching a burning car to rescue your child — or any other person — where you burn yourself severely in the process. How would you regard your injuries? With a sense of relief, even satisfaction that you saved them? With pride, because you didn't shy away from the danger?

This brings up the distinction between pain and suffering. The more your focus is driven by emotions, the more intense the suffering. Many research findings suggest that attaching an emotion to a painful event turns pain into suffering.

By now you'll probably guess why this is the case. Emotions are irrational, fickle and have no sense of time and place. Therefore, they are all encompassing and endless when we experience them. When attached to the experience of pain it means that it too becomes 'boundless' and increasingly unbearable.

Conclusion: while pain may be unavoidable, suffering is optional.

Rather than resorting to drugs, which can only provide temporary relief in most cases, and which also carry the danger of leading to dependency and addiction, by making use of the brain's ability to change, this neuroplasticity promises much greater and longer lasting relief.

As is the case for any body part, the old maxim 'use it or lose it' holds true. When in pain we tend to protect what hurts, we use it less and less, which of course, means we eventually lose its use altogether, because muscles waste away, tendons become tight, and every move becomes more painful. At the same time the neural connections in the brain linked to the particular body part also wither away through disuse and recovery is increasingly less likely as the sufferer settles into their fate.

Breaking this identification with the 'disability' and drawing a line around what is (physically) not possible and what can still be achieved means you now experience a new sense of control. Rather than focusing on the restrictions, turn to extending the range of what you *can* do. Each small increase in mobility means a little more control over your life. Remember the 'jnd' — you might not immediately notice the difference, but as you learn to pick things up off the floor again, touch your knees and then your toes you'll notice your control returning. BUT *gently* does it every time!

I know from my personal experience of restrictions and pain, it can be a big task to move from a 'victim' mentality to acceptance where, yes, you're restricted but that doesn't define you. Unless you let it, and let it run — and ruin — your life.

Call it wilful acceptance, which means you exercise control by choosing to accept rather than fight a battle you can't win, and you'll notice having more control means less stress.

Please don't consider this as a complete guide to controlling chronic pain, but an encouragement not to necessarily equate pain with suffering. To successfully relieve pain you may have to combine these suggestions with other forms of therapy. Controlled and focused breathing, mindfulness and meditation, gentle stretching exercises and starting a gentle (!) but regular physical activity regime, which you then slowly increase as your abilities improve, may all be part of the recovery, or pain management process.

13. Potholes on the elusive road to happiness

I trust that by now you'll agree with how far reaching the implications are if you accept that you can't control anything outside yourself. The next step will only be a minor one, because it's the logical extension of the same premise. When it comes to the pursuit of happiness, and finding happiness, there is little point (make that no point) in searching. It's nowhere to be found out there.

It makes sense when people suggest a definition of happiness as being a state of mind. It's not an event, nor a feeling, but a pervasive sense of contentment that comes with being alive. Imagine a fictitious person we define as being happy. Now imagine you asked them at any given time 'Are you happy right now?' The answer is likely to be a moment of silence. This 'happy' person would have to consider the way they feel at *that* point in time, and would probably not come up with a particular reason for why they would be happy.

Yet, if you asked them are they happy with their life they may nonetheless agree. A boundary focus has no problem accepting this and, in fact, wouldn't even try to identify or define happiness and how to achieve it. As such it agrees with many of the principles of positive psychology, and encourages the search within, rather than suggesting the search outside of the self for the cause, or the source, of happiness.

Other than making the mistake of searching for happiness 'in the world', in material things or through fulfilment in relationships, there are two further potholes or pitfalls on the road to becoming and being yourself. There's always a risk involved when talking in superlatives and extremes. Although I'm tempted to take that risk, temptation is tempered with prudence and (you might say, emotions tempered with reason) I'll simply call the following two potholes examples that are often the cause of much grief, stress and angst.

No boundaries? Default mechanism to the rescue

To highlight why this is a pothole let me quickly recap and expand a little on brain activity and the importance of early childhood experiences.

After the foundations have been laid for the young brain, shaped by its experiences, every other event then strengthens an accustomed response pattern, helping the child to negotiate the world and shaping its expectations. Eventually the sum of these experiences and the way the child responds become part of what we later regard as the person's personality, or their default mechanism.

Neuroplasticity allows us to change our habitual responses through acts of will, insight or as the result of thinking before acting. However, when we're subjected exceedingly to stressors we find difficult to accommodate, we find ourselves reverting to behaviour patterns (call them habits if you want) we thought we'd abandoned eons ago. We start to display our childhood reactions. The brain just doesn't seem to forget these deeply engrained patterns, even after a very long time.

The relevance for the issue of boundaries is fundamental. The reversion to childhood behaviour occurs when the person didn't experience 'boundaries' when they were a child, in the sense that their emotional experiences were associated and confined to a particular situation. If the emotional experience is re-experienced, albeit as an adult and in different circumstances, we respond as if still that child of old.

Poorly maintained boundaries

Another reason for the reversion to infantile behaviour can be seen when boundaries were only vaguely defined or randomly maintained during childhood. The child learns that Daddy is angry, not because of a particular event or because something didn't go according to plan, but always and unpredictably so. The situation becomes even more unbearable for the child, if it perceives itself as the cause. The effect is not unlike what we know about post-traumatic stress, and the pervasive unsettling expectation that the unpleasant event is recurring or will recur at any moment. The effect is that any emotion isn't limited to the situation that created it, but is 'boundless'. It transcends the situation and threatens to become ever-present — like setting a beginning but no end time.

In adults we often see the result of this in the tendency to rehash past events. Any argument about a current situation tends to turn into a history lesson of past mistakes and an account of who said what, when, and how often. It's the inability to draw a line around past events, and stay with the issue at hand. Sound familiar?

From early childhood on we try to learn about the connection between cause and effect so we can make inferences about the future. This in turn makes our small world predictable and, thereby, that little bit safer. Not having to be concerned about its safety, an infant is now able to play, explore its environment and establish its place in the wider world. Even if the expected consequences are adverse, it can predict what's going to happen and take precautions, for example, by hiding under the blanket or bed and try to become invisible — and feel safer for the illusion.

The amygdala is not only quite primitive, it has no sense of reality. When it's turned on, it fires and sets in motion a number of reactions, which result in the system being alarmed and armed. It doesn't matters if the threat is real or imagined; once the amygdala is alarmed the threat *is* real.

So why does it go off over trivial things such as a scary movie we know isn't real? These days our reason for existence isn't simply 'survival and procreation'. In the developed world, we now have the luxury to pursue a variety of goals as important as reducing our golf handicap or going dancing on the weekend, and we drive cars not simply for transport but also for pleasure. Work is no longer simply for survival. We can derive pleasure from it and use the proceeds not simply for food but to acquire superfluous items unnecessary for survival.

Remember, though, once we make the decision we 'must' have them, such items are deemed essential by the right brain. We're now dealing with the irrational 'infant' who wants, absolutely needs, and who doesn't want to hear the word 'no' and takes what it can get, if it can get away with it. Most importantly, it does not 'consider'— least of all the consequences. And I'm not talking about teenagers here. That's the right brain for you!

This behaviour is inherent in all of us well beyond our teenage years. The difference between feeling a desire and acting on it is that we've learned or have been taught through more or less painful lessons, which in turn influenced our actions, that wanting is OK, but pursuing and getting it may be another matter. That process is not confined to, but generally occurs throughout childhood and adolescence. At some point, though, we're expected to control our desires and impulses. It's what makes us different from the animal world.

What we want is also what we need, according to the right brain. Full stop! There's no such thing as trivial when it comes to what our right brain wants. Just ask any child. What is important and what is not is a decision based on rational considerations by comparing one value with another, taking the situation and circumstances into account and whatever else we do when we make rational decisions. This different appreciation of an event also explains the varied reactions different people have to the same event. Take the result of a football match that literally devastates a dedicated follower, but for the rational commentator is simply material to discuss and analyze dispassionately.

A boundary focus is only a first step. If it takes you where you feel comfortable and you experience no difficulties, you've got it made! If however, you find it hard or sometimes impossible to recognize or accept boundaries, you may want to explore the reasons. That would be the time to speak with someone outside your comfort zone, a counsellor or psychologist or person who is able to establish and maintain boundaries. However, while you may be ready on a cognitive level, only if you feel safe that these boundaries are observed will you be able to go further down the path of self-discovery and identify the events that prevent you from accepting your own boundaries. And that means *accepting* yourself.

14. **The panacea of sorts: 'me time'**

How do we give ourselves a break from feelings of guilt, revenge, anger or any of the more negative aspects in our memory bank that seem to haunt us, some of which even follow us into sleep and cause ill feelings about ourselves and others?

Let me remind you: whenever we do something we rely on the availability of energy, which the body has to supply. This 'energy surge' is released in a variety of actions, which are then labelled and related back to the emotions we assume drove the action.

While the expression of emotions may differ and vary, so that being angry can result in a violent outburst on one occasion and in a fit of tearful desperation on another, the nature of emotions does not change. Underlying any emotion are physiological processes, which lead to a build-up of physical energy. Energy that is not released is accumulated and has one of two options; it can go either outwards or inwards, meaning you eventually turn on someone else or yourself.

It's no coincidence that the widely accepted first line of defence against depression is not medication; it's (drum roll) physical activity. Movement, mobilizing the system, using the introverted energy and directing it outward is the best defence. In studies, psychotherapeutic interventions have also been found to be far superior to medications and show longer-lasting positive effects in helping individuals manage their depression.

I use the phrase 'physical activity' and not 'exercise' to emphasize that the aim is not to lose weight or increase fitness. These are only by-products. Importantly, during at least moderately strenuous physical activity endorphins are released. These are the body's feel-good chemicals, a naturally produced opiate derivative, which incidentally also helps to conquer pain. Together with the release of adrenaline, serotonin and dopamine, which are involved in the feelings of reward, general wellbeing and 'feeling good', endorphins are a powerful anti-depressant. In other words, when you feel on top of the world, you can thank the effects of these chemicals.

Another reason I prefer to use 'physical activity' is the association with pressure we often feel when we hear the word exercise, as in *I should be exercising more* and *It's good for you*. As everybody knows, what feels good is often also difficult to do, expensive or forbidden. Therefore, choose an activity you're comfortable with, if not outright love, be it jogging, brisk walking, long-distance running, pushbike riding, swimming, paddling, rowing — whatever. If nothing springs to mind, pick something that comes closest to some buried interest. Start slowly to overcome any aversion, and the possible fear it may kill you (like Mr Churchill who claimed 'Sport is murder'), and slowly build up the time you spend doing it.

If the activity doesn't interest you too much, the following might grab your attention. Use this time as your 'me-time', the time when you don't have to talk or listen to anybody else, where you have no phone to answer, nobody to look after or answer to. You can dream, think, fantasize. (I regularly prepare myself for winning the lottery.) Do whatever floats your boat, or rather keeps your legs going.

After a while you'll simply crave the time set aside for yourself. Do it on a regular basis (you're worth it!) and do it for at least 45 minutes or, better still, an hour (I need at least that time to spend the money I won in my virtual lottery), if you can squeeze it out of your day. It's the time of the day when you belong to yourself. If you're a busy mum, make time for yourself. Get a babysitter, or get hubby, enlist your mother, mother-in-law or friend. Stop looking for excuses *not* to do it, look for ways to *do* it. (Think 'want' not 'should'.) To keep things interesting you can also add variety by alternating between different activities on different days. On the endurance scale from 0 to 10 (0 = being asleep, 10 = just shy of a heart attack) do it on a level between 6 and 8.

Let your emotions loose

Apart from the release of endorphins that make you feel good, this is now also the time when you can do your worrying, if you so choose. You can be angry, plan revenge attacks in your mind or indulge in whatever other fantasies.

Why is it all of a sudden OK to let your emotions loose? Emotions equate to energy. As you build up your emotions (energy level), you release them at the same time through your physical activity. This leaves your (left) brain free to do some thinking without being distracted by emotional interference. In fact, if you've established a routine of a regular daily activity, you can tell yourself during the day that you have no time to get distracted by your anger or worries right now, and you'll think about that vexing issue 'tonight, when I go for my run'. This is a useful strategy for putting thoughts into their place, and importantly, to allocate them a time when it suits you to attend to them. Who's running this show anyway? You think about it when it pleases you, not your thoughts. Put your foot down!

If you do your activity before you get comfortable at home — that is, right after returning from work — the additional benefit is that the stress you've accumulated over the day stays outside your home. When you come back again, you're really home! Now you can relax, play with the kids, talk to your partner and deal with whatever you have to without 'blowing up'. (You won't have the energy anymore.)

Doing physical activity before coming home is a way to avoid conflict, which often only arises because of 'stress' — the energy level that's built up over the course of the day. Releasing it through physical activity obviously prevents it being released towards family members, including the dog.

Take a deep breath

How often have you heard that, and wanted to hit the person making the suggestion? Now let me tell you why you might get annoyed and also, why I suggest you do it — the deep breathing that is, not hitting the person! Deep breathing is just as effective as physical activity to control emotions and you don't even have to leave your seat to do it.

Part 1 explained how energy is produced when we perceive a threat. In the first instance we change our breathing because it provides the necessary oxygen, which then triggers further changes such as increased blood pressure and heart rate, etc. In a simplistic way you could say that the more oxygen we have, the more energy we have available. This may explain why you became more aggressive when you 'took a deep breath' sometimes with the added suggestion to 'count to ten'. As you take in more oxygen, you increase your oxygen level and therefore by the time you reach ten, you're well and truly ready to punch someone's lights out. Why do I suggest, then, that breathing helps you to calm down?

When being chased by a wild dog and you get tired, are you going to lie down and have a bit of a snooze because you feel so tired? Hardly. You rest only once you make it to safety. In the meantime, you increase your breathing rate until the threat is over. If you don't make it, the story ends here. Alternatively, you make it to safety and, protected by your folks or a solid door, you can now lie down, rest and sleep. During (healthy) sleep we naturally change from breathing into the top of the lungs to breathing down into the diaphragm. The effect is reduced oxygen in your system because the slower breathing rate allows the body to re-establish the balance between oxygen and carbon dioxide, and less oxygen means less energy — hey presto, you feel relaxed. No magic, just physiology working for you.

Because you normally only breathe into the diaphragm when you sleep, it indicates to the brain that you must be safe, since you wouldn't lie down to sleep if you weren't. Consequently, if you're not threatened there's no need for stress hormones, so the brain stops initiating the release of adrenaline and cortisol. Together with the reduction of oxygen in your system, it slows down and you feel more relaxed.

Getting into the habit of taking a few diaphragmatic breaths on a regular basis during the day — for example, every time you sit down at your desk, pass the water dispenser or sit down for a meal — has the effect of you releasing accumulated adrenaline. Instead of allowing it to build up and 'stress you', you get rid of it. You'll notice how your shoulders drop, and calmness takes over, then you can resume your normal activities. It only takes a second. OK, thirty seconds.

The effect is this: when we don't control it, 'stress' builds up and becomes increasingly difficult to calm down again.

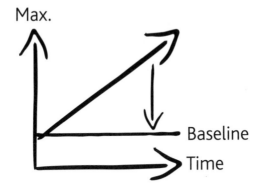

Taking diaphragmatic breaths reduces stress built-up:

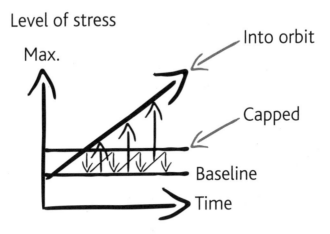

As you can see, what causes your stress level to rise doesn't change, but your stress level is capped instead of shooting into orbit. This is one example of when it sounds too good to be true it's actually not.

Breathing exercise

You may have encountered this exercise in various guises already and essentially it's meant to help you slow down your breathing, however, I've adapted it slightly — for good reason.

Place a hand on your stomach and push out the air, keeping up a bit of pressure to remind you that this is where you want the air to go when you breathe in. Place the other hand on your chest. While breathing in through your nose focus on the feeling of the air as it touches the inside of your nostrils and then moves through your sinus area. Now feel your stomach muscles expand as you breathe into your diaphragm. While the hand on your stomach rises, the one on your chest shouldn't move.

Breathe out through your nose, very slowly (this is very important!) at about half the speed you breathed in. As you breathe out, feel the stomach muscles relax, and then pick up the airflow again, as it brushes against the inside of your nostrils. Then repeat as many times as you like or have time for.

The breathing rhythm is 'stomach in and out', not the chest going up and down. If you find it difficult at first, do it when you lie in bed before you go to sleep. It's easier when you're lying flat on your back (remember, this is the way you naturally breathe when you're asleep). Falling asleep during or after this exercise also ensures you're relaxed, rather than exhausted.

Don't do this when you're tired and driving a car, or doing any other activity that requires your full attention, since you may fall asleep. Otherwise, you can do this as often as you like during the day. It helps you control your level of arousal and is, therefore, useful as a means of 'anger management' or 'energy management' as you may want to call it from now on.

No sleep — no good

You could argue that sleep has nothing to do with boundaries. While this may be so, it's also a fact that without proper sleep it's very difficult to think straight and change good intention into reality. Don't take your lead from Sir Winston Churchill, who reportedly only slept about four hours a night. He's also well known for fighting the 'black dog', as he called his depression.

Sleep consists of regular 'deep' sleep, including the REM (rapid eye movement) phase when you dream. During this phase the hippocampus in the limbic system, where we store short-term emotional memories, discharges and clears the mind's RAM (Random Access Memory), to use a computer analogy. Studies have shown that if you don't give it enough time to 'clear', you wake up still feeling tired. Small wonder that you then find it difficult to take in new information, focus and function.

If you wake up tired in the morning you haven't slept enough, or not properly. Don't just count the hours; make sure you get 'good' sleep. This means going through four phases of REM sleep — the last one obviously being the one we miss out on. Have you ever turned around after the alarm clock went off, pressed 'snooze', only to wake again, generally being 'late' now, but feeling really refreshed? Add that time to your sleep by going to bed earlier.

It seems almost unnecessary to add that shift work doesn't lend itself to healthy sleep habits. In fact, it's probably at the root of many problems shift workers face, be they mental-health related or with their relationships. When it's unavoidable and you have to submit to the necessity of shift work, it's even more important to minimize the risks of unhealthy sleep patterns.

If you're concerned speak to your doctor or a psychologist, who may guide you to a good night's sleep. Silly as it may sound, we can acquire bad sleep habits. The good news is we can also learn to sleep well again through a process called sleep hygiene. This is of particular importance for shift workers, who have to be extra vigilant when it comes to their sleep.

Thoughts are just that

Worry thoughts can strike anytime, whether we're awake or asleep, since they originate in our brain, and that never sleeps. When you're asleep they can wake you up, and during the day, they can give rise to anxiety.

When worry thoughts do arise, give them a time when you choose to attend to them. Rather than trying not to think about them, address the thoughts and decide when you'll think about what frightens you. If you're engaged in a regular physical activity routine as I suggested earlier, this would be a good time. Instead of thinking *I don't want to think about this*, say to yourself *I don't want to think about this **now**, I'll think about it tomorrow in my 'me-time'.* Also remind yourself of the fact that thoughts are just that — thoughts. They can't hurt you! They're only in your head. Whatever you make out of a situation, it only occurs in your own mind.

Moreover, it's not the thought that keeps you awake, it's the emotion it evokes. You can treat any thought simply as a 'thinking exercise', like a movie playing in front of your mental eye. You don't have to become involved in the movie. Simply let it run and observe. Decide that you now could get emotional at a particular point, but you decide *not* to, and instead go back to sleep.

During the day, it may suffice to remind yourself that a thought can't hurt you. As far as your rational brain is concerned, it makes no difference if you think about your grocery list or how you felt when you felt you embarrassed yourself. In either case it's only a matter of neurons firing. That's all. The feeling that this firing evokes happens in a totally different and much more primitive part of your brain.

The only way to curb that emotional activity is through the engagement of the rational area of the brain. This is the case for any emotion. Left unbridled, there's no telling where it'll take you.

Relaxation exercise

Should you wake up during the night, or find it difficult to fall asleep, try progressive muscle relaxation. Focus on each individual muscle in your body, starting with your feet and working your way up to the top your head. Contract then relax every muscle you come across, one at a time. Then stretch it in the opposite direction and relax. You may be surprised at all the muscles you may discover and never thought you had.

As an alternative, imagine your feet, then legs, then arms, then head and so on, getting very, very heavy. After ten seconds let them become very light.

You can also use the alternation of cold and hot. Any of the opposites will do. But always finish with the light or warm feeling, to end on a pleasant note.

References

Ainsworth, M.D.S., Blehar, M. C., Waters, E., & Wall, S. (1978). *Patterns of Attachment: A psychological study of the strange situation.* Oxford, UK: Earlbaum

Bowlby, J. (1972). *Child Care and the Growth of Love.* Middlesex, GB: Penguin Books

Bowlby, J. (1988). *A Secure Base: Parent–child attachment and healthy human development.* New York: Basic Books Inc

Cozolino, L. (2006). *The Neuroscience of Human Development: Attachment and the developing social brain.* New York: W.W. Norton & Company

Descartes, René (1644). *The Principles of Philosophy (IX, X).* Translated from the Latin by John Veitch

Dieter, H.G. (2010). *Creating Criminals Without Even Trying.* Burleigh, Qld: Zeus Publications

Doidge, N. (2007). *The Brain That Changes Itself.* New York: Penguin Group

Gershon, M. (1998) *The Second Brain.* New York: HarperCollins Publishers

Greenspan, S.I., Shankar, S.G. (2004). *The First Idea.* Cambridge, MA: DaCapo Press

Hawking, S. (1988). *A Brief History of Time*. Sydney, NSW: Bantam Books

Iacoboni, M. (2008). *Mirroring People*. Farrar. New York: Strauss and Giroux

Josef, R. (1992). *The Right Brain and the Unconscious*. New York, NY: Plenum Press

Kandel, E.R. (1998). 'A New Intellectual Framework for Psychiatry'. *American Journal of Psychiatry*, 155, pp. 457–469.

LeBaron, M. (2003). 'Culture-Based Negotiation Styles'. *Beyond Intractability*. Ed. Guy Burgess and Heidi Burgess. Conflict Research Consortium, University of Colorado, Boulder, Colorado, USA. Posted July 2003 http://www.beyondintractability.org/essay/culture-negotiatio

MacLean, P.D. (1990). *The Triune Brain in Evolution: Role in Paleocerebral Functions*. New York: Plenum Press

Manger, T.A. Motta, R.W. (2005). 'The Impact of an Exercise Program on Post-traumatic Stress Disorder, Anxiety and Depression'. *International Journal of Emergency Mental Health*, 7, pp. 49–57.

Merzenich, M.M. (1983). 'Topographic Reorganization of Somatosensory Cortical aAeas 3b qd 1 in Adult Monkeys Following Restricted Deafferentation', *Neuroscience*, 8, pp. 33–55.

Merzenich, M. (2013). *Softwired: How the new science of brain plasticity can change your life*. San Francisco: Parnassus Publishing.

Montgomery, A. (2013). *Neurobiology essentials for clinicians*. New York: W.W. Norton & Co.

Phelps, E.A. (2004).' Human Emotion and Memory: Interactions of the amygdala and hippocampal complex'. *Current Opinion in Neurobiology*, 14, pp. 198–202

Pritchard, R. (1996). *Love in the Real World*. Auckland: Penguin Books

Ross, H.E. and Murray, D. J. (1996). (Ed. and Transl.) *E.H. Weber on the Tactile Senses*. 2nd ed. Hove, UK: Erlbaum Taylor & Francis

Roussow, P. J. (2010). *The Neurobiological Underpinnings of the Mental Health Renaissance*. 20th Annual Mental Health Services Conference Inc. of Australia and New Zealand. 14–17 September 2010. Sydney, Aus.

Rossouw, P.J. (ed.) (2014). *Neuropsychotherapy. Theoretical underpinnings and clinical applications*. Sydney: Mediros.

Schore, A. N. (2003). *Affect Regulation and the Repair of the Self*. New York: W.W. Norton & Company

Siegel, D. (1999). *The Developing Mind: Toward a neurobiology of interpersonal experience*. New York: Guilford Press

Stacey R.D. (2003). *Strategic Management and Organisational Dynamics: The challenge of complexity*. Essex, UK: Pearson Education

Steptoe, A., Hamer, M. & Chida, Y. (2005). 'The Effects of Acute Psychological Stress on Circulating Inflammatory Factors in Humans: A review and meta-analysis'. *Brain, Behavior, and Immunity, Vol. 21, Issue 7*, October 2007, pp. 901–912

Van der Kolk, B.A. (2006). *Clinical Implications of Neuroscience Research in PTSD*, Annual of the New York Academy of Science July, Volume 1071, pp. 277–293

Weiss, J. M. (1968). 'Effects of Coping Responses on Stress'. *Journal of Comparative and Physiological Psychology Vol. 65*, No. 2, pp. 251–260

White, B.L. (1995). *New First Three Years of Life*. New York, NY: Fireside

Wright, K. (1991). *Vision and Separation between Mother and Baby*. Northvale NJ: Jason Aronson Inc.

Index